PENGUIN BOOKS

WIN-WIN CAREER NEGOTIATIONS

Peter Goodman is a nationally known specialist on careers and job-search issues. His company, MyJobCoach, Inc., is a comprehensive on-line career resource for people in job transition, and has been featured in *The Wall Street Journal*, *The Washington Post*, *BusinessWeek*, and the *Chicago Tribune*, among other leading national publications.

Goodman has more than ten years of experience fusing employment needs with technology. He has founded several organizations, including MSI Software, Inc., a medical staffing software development company. As the president and CEO for seven years, he led this company to market leadership, servicing clients such as Harvard, Johns Hopkins, UCLA Medical Center, Cornell, and an additional 1,200 major healthcare institutions. His earlier launch, University Scholarship Publications, Inc., was an innovative advertising/marketing operation targeting university students.

Win–Win Career Negotiations

Proven Strategies for Getting What You Want from Your Employer

Peter J. Goodman

PENGUIN BOOKS

To my grandparents,
Wladimir and Martha Selinsky,
who taught me that anything is possible
if you put your mind to it.

PENGUIN BOOKS
Published by the Penguin Group
Penguin Putnam Inc., 375 Hudson Street, New York, New York 10014, U.S.A.
Penguin Books Ltd, 80 Strand, London WC2R 0RL, England
Penguin Books Australia Ltd, 250 Camberwell Road, Camberwell, Victoria 3124, Australia
Penguin Books Canada Ltd, 10 Alcorn Avenue, Toronto, Ontario, Canada M4V 3B2
Penguin Books India (P) Ltd, 11 Community Centre,
Panchsheel Park, New Delhi – 110 017, India
Penguin Books (N.Z.) Ltd, Cnr Rosedale and Airborne Roads,
Albany, Auckland, New Zealand
Penguin Books (South Africa) (Pty) Ltd, 24 Sturdee Avenue,
Rosebank, Johannesburg 2196, South Africa

Penguin Books Ltd, Registered Offices:
Harmondsworth, Middlesex, England

First published in the United States of America by Gut Instinct Press 2001
Published in Penguin Books 2002

10 9 8 7 6 5 4 3 2 1

THE LIBRARY OF CONGRESS HAS CATALOGED
THE GUT INSTINCT PRESS EDITION AS FOLLOWS:
Goodman, Peter J.
Win-win career negotiations : all you need to know about
negotiating your employment agreement / Peter J. Goodman. — 1st ed.
p. cm.
Includes index.
LCCN 2001118694
ISBN 0-9713907-4-6 (Gut Instinct Press)
ISBN 0 14 20.0251 8 (Penguin Books)
1. Career development. 2. Negotiations in business. 3. Labor contract. I. Title.
HF5549.5.C35G66 2001 650.14
QB101-201237

Printed in the United States of America
Designed by Stephanie Deveau

Contents

Acknowledgments

This book began with the idea that there is an enormous need to open up the topic of negotiations for the job candidate. Through our research and interviews with many individuals, ranging from recent college graduates to senior-level executives, we identified the topics that pose challenges during the job negotiation process, then prepared ways to address these topics.

I must first thank Roger Fisher, who teaches negotiations at Harvard Law School, where he is director of the Harvard Negotiation Project. Professor Fisher has generously shared with me his time and passion for the topic of negotiations. In addition, the landmark book *Getting to YES,* by Roger Fisher, William Ury, and Bruce Patton, provided the inspiration and framework for the principles and strategies described in this guide.

I am also grateful to my colleagues, friends, and attorneys—Roy Morris, Phil Schwartz, and Tim Feely—who contributed so much to the guide. Each has provided valuable information about the world of collaborative career negotiations. My particular appreciation goes to Tom Goodwin, who contributed his time and offered access to his network of business and political leaders. In addition, I wish to recognize Alvah Parker, Cynthia Stringer, and Don Weintraub, three outstanding executive career coaches, who gave me an insider's view of various corporate environments.

Special thanks go to my business partner, colleague, and friend, Richard Ashodian, whose twenty years of experience in the career industry and understanding of the psychology of the job seeker have made this project both possible and fun. My gratitude is extended to Jennifer Zaslow, David Gumpert, Alesia Benedict, Laurie Johnston, Margery Niblock, and Sunder Aaron, whose insights contributed to this book. My particular thanks go to Kate O'Halloran, who guided me in the editorial process.

Finally, I would like to thank my parents, Lori and Stephen Goodman, and my family, whose support over the years has given me the strength and confidence to pursue one entrepreneurial endeavor after another. Their support throughout each challenge has helped me realize why it's all worth it in the end.

—Peter J. Goodman

Foreword

Looking for a new job can be highly stressful. You go to an interview with well-ironed clothes and a well-scrubbed face hoping to answer without hesitation whatever questions the interviewer asks. Too often, the questions seem dull and routine (as do your answers). Most of the information was there in your resume—which the interviewer apparently skimmed. Or are those questions being asked deliberately to see how you react? Yes, negotiating a job interview can be a challenge.

Yet a job interview is also a wonderful opportunity to meet somebody in the organization where you might work. You would like to learn more about the potential job and about people there. And you would like to have someone there learn more about you.

This book is an excellent guide, full of ideas and information that you should have in your head as you sit down to negotiate. It is particulary strong in important areas where I, personally, am weak, such as precedents and criteria regarding stock options, bonus plans, benefits, a noncompete clause, a severance package, and the actual text of an employment agreement. I urge you to read this book, read it carefully, and then read it again. A wise student once told me that he had learned three important things from our negogiation workshop, "prepare…prepare…and prepare."

What can I add? As Peter Goodman cautions you, keep the big picture in mind. In a job negotiation, as in most others, you and those with whom you are dealing are not adversaries. As you move toward an agreement, you will find that you disagree on a number of issues. Many of them will be financial. It is easy to disagree about money. You are, however, potential colleagues, working together as joint problem solvers.

For you, the desired outcome of this negotiation is twofold. You would like to learn enough about the organization, the people who work there, what they do and how they do it, to convince you that this, above all other options, is the place where you would like to work. You would like to come away with a well-founded, enthusiastic interest in having a job there.

Your second goal is to have the interviewer become enthusiastic about you, and to know enough about you to be able to persuade others in the organization that you should be offered such a good job that you would be certain to accept.

In a job interview, as in courtship, the major interests of both sides are identical. The best outcome is one in which both sides are enthusiastic, optimistic, and even excited about the prospect of a new relationship. Financial and other practical aspects are certainly important, but they are all secondary to achieving an emotional commitment on both sides to go forward together. Negotiating over a future job, like most negotiations, is a joint search for a good outcome.

Much of this book is written for people who are already fairly certain that they want this particular job. Whether or not that is the case, my advice is not just to sit in an interview waiting for the next question. Asking good questions yourself is often the best way to gather more data as well as to demonstrate your competence: "Why is this job open? Is it a new position, or did the previous employee get promoted? Transferred? Fired? Leave? Might it be a good idea for me to talk with him or her, or with others who might become my colleagues?" "What has been your experience with turnover?" "If I don't get this job, what other companies in town would you think might be the best place for me to work? Why? How does your company compare with them?" "Are superiors in this organization, as well as colleagues and subordinates, likely to give me enough feedback, coaching, and other advice, if I ask for it, to make it possible for me to continue to build and refine my management skills?" "If I work evenings and weekends, am I likely to find myself alone in the office?"

Asking questions does not mean that you dominate an interview. By asking good questions you are likely to reveal more of your abilities than by merely answering routine questions. And don't forget to listen.

Enjoy this book. And learn to enjoy negotiating a new job.

—Roger Fisher
Director, Harvard Negotiation Project

Introduction

Everyone knows what the word "negotiations" means, but most of us are uncomfortable with the process; we don't know the best way to engage in successful negotiations. The negotiation process seems mysterious and fearful. However, in everyday life, we negotiate successfully all the time, whether it's figuring out what movie to see with a friend or deciding what restaurant to go to. Each of these situations involves many different decisions, emotions, and feelings, as well as collaborative reasoning and compromise in order to reach a mutually acceptable outcome.

For example, imagine that you and a friend are trying to decide where to eat; you are in the mood for Italian food, but your friend is not. You probably don't keep listing Italian restaurants for your friend to reject. Instead, you try to get the other person engaged in the decision-making process: "What do you think? Where would you like to go?"

When you ask your friend to make suggestions, you increase the chances of finding an acceptable restaurant and reaching a compromise that results in mutual satisfaction. Although this situation involves an initial disagreement, through one party's willingness to consider the other's needs, the outcome is agreeable to both parties.

Whether it's negotiating where to eat or negotiating a complex business deal, the most important thing to remember is that people are involved on both sides of the process. If you can work with people and can empathize—whether or not you agree—with their positions, you already have a basic understanding of what's involved in the negotiating process.

This guide will help you develop and expand on that basic understanding so that you can negotiate successfully in a variety of situations, focusing on the career development process. We will start with the basic skills any negotiator needs, and then show you how to apply those skills to negotiating each element of the hiring process, from employment agreements through salary, bonuses, severance packages, annual reviews, and on-the-job negotiations with co-workers.

The Win–Win career negotiations process incorporates the approach described in *Getting to YES: Negotiating Agreements Without Giving In,* by Roger Fisher, William Ury, and Bruce Patton. In their book, Fisher, Ury, and Patton identify two different types of negotiation, principled negotiation and positional negotiation. In *positional negotiation,* each party takes a firm position and tries to convince the other to compromise. Both parties have a top or bottom figure in mind, but they keep that figure secret. The "negotiation" consists of each party making a series of concessions that moves them closer to their bottom-line figure, while trying to move the other party closer to his or her bottom line. At the end of the process, the person who has stayed closest to the opening position "wins."

In *principled negotiation,* the process is collaborative, not adversarial. The negotiation is seen as being mutually beneficial for both parties. In terms of the hiring process, principled negotiation involves looking at the negotiation from both parties' perspectives. The company has made a considerable investment in the hiring process; they want the person they hire to feel positive about the job, and about the company. If you go into the negotiations process with this perspective in mind, you increase the likelihood of reaching an agreement that will satisfy both parties.

Our goal is to illustrate how to make career negotiations a win–win proposition, rather than a poker game proposition of bluff and double-bluff. By understanding and embracing the techniques described in this guide, you will greatly increase your chances of resolving a variety of negotiations and conflicts.

To effectively apply the principles in this book, practice these three strategies: (1) become aware of situations that require these techniques and skills; (2) think about both your goals and those of the other party before any negotiation or discussion; and (3) practice following the techniques to become comfortable with the process, and to become familiar with the challenges associated with understanding the other party's interests.

The more you train yourself to define your interests, then anticipate the interests of the other party, the more confident and in control you will feel. This new attitude will naturally carry forward and will benefit you in building new relationships and in improving existing relationships, both professional and personal.

In the guide, the core approach is applied to various aspects of interviewing, hiring, and on the job, which are then illustrated through real-life experiences of leading executives and business professionals. It is our hope that this collective work will provide you with added insight into a topic that is unfamiliar to many.

We start with an overview of the negotiation process and the skills that are essential for negotiating success. Then, in Part Two, we address the specifics of negotiating the different elements of the hiring and career development process.

If you are already familiar with the basics, you may want to go straight to Part Two, or to move back and forth between sections. Whatever your approach, we hope you will find this guide a useful companion in the negotiation process. Part Three looks at the big picture of negotiations, with insights from two experienced negotiators and a look at the negotiations of the everyday working world. Finally, the Appendix presents a flawed employment agreement for your analysis.

PART ONE

Introduction to Negotiations

CHAPTER ONE

The Essentials of Negotiation

Like it or not, you are a negotiator.
Negotiation is a fact of life.
—Roger Fisher, William Ury, and
Bruce Patton, *Getting to YES*

What is the difference between *negotiation* and *successful negotiation*? Often, it is nothing more than developing good communication skills, using them to keep the negotiation collaborative, and preparing thoroughly for the three stages of negotiations. In this chapter, we will begin by looking at the skills used by successful negotiators, the four areas in which these skills are applied, and the three stages that all negotiations can be broken down into.

Negotiating Skills

Some people seem to be born negotiators. The girl who can stop a fight over the most desirable swing on the playground becomes the woman who defuses a potential labor union strike. However, the skills needed for most negotiations can be learned. While we may not all be able to negotiate, say, a peace treaty among the major world powers, we can all develop the skills for successful negotiations at the individual level. Whether the negotiation involves a child's playground or nuclear arms, the skills needed remain the same: *listening, communication, self-control,* and *focus.* You can increase your mastery of each of these skills, and thus increase your abilities as a negotiator.

Listening

Have you ever had a conversation with someone in which you used the other person's talk-time to prepare a response to what was being said, rather than actually listening to it? Many people tend to make this mistake. We are concerned with presenting ourselves as intelligent and articulate. Spending the time to plan the structure of our response, and the way it is worded, should help keep us from getting tied up in sentences that go nowhere. Unfortunately, this may make us sound articulate, but it doesn't necessarily make us sound intelligent. Instead of using the other person's talk-time to work on your phrasing, use it to really understand what is being said. When you actually hear what others are saying, you are able to understand their perceptions, and their point of view. This prevents misinterpretation and enables you to tailor what you say to their perspectives. Also, when others know they are being heard, they are more likely to perceive you in a positive light. Here are some simple techniques to improve your listening skills:

- Pay close attention to what the other person is saying.
- If you find that something the other person said is unclear, ask to have it repeated.
- As you listen, work on understanding how the other person sees himself or herself.
- Acknowledge what the other person is saying, and demonstrate that you understand it, by repeating the idea in your own words.

Communication

Clear communication is essential to successful negotiation, not only because it lets you explain your point of view during the negotiation itself, but also because it helps you gain insights into the other person's perspective. To engage in successful job negotiations, it's important for both parties to understand each other's interests. You can do this if you ask questions, interpret and understand what they're saying and why, then respond to their statements. Remember, communication is a two-way process. Don't just speak; listen. And when you do speak, make sure your focus is on being understood. This is a discussion, not a debate; you don't score points for showing that the other person's logic is faulty. Focus the discussion on the other person's needs. This keeps him or her interested in what you have to say, which helps you achieve your objectives.

It's also important to be aware of nonverbal communication, both your own and the other person's. The way you present yourself affects the impression you make on the other person. To a trained observer, body language can give a lot of information about your responses during negotiations. One successful negotiator describes a post-negotiation discussion where he learned that the other party had trained as a psychologist, specializing in nonverbal communication. Throughout the negotiation, the other man had a very clear picture of the negotiator's reactions to issues, based on his body language. Make sure your body language is communicating the right messages: confidence and security.

Self-control

Throughout the negotiations process, it's important to remain consistent and to separate personal emotions from the process. If you begin to react on an emotional level, both your professional appearance and your effectiveness suffer.

Keep in mind that people of different behavioral styles may have different ways of expressing and processing information. If you feel you are not conveying your points successfully, you may have to adjust your method of communication. For example, a sales-oriented negotiator might be animated, fluid with speech, use hand gestures, and offer few specifics, whereas an engineering-oriented negotiator might approach the discussion from a more analytical and detailed perspective. Neither approach is wrong; however, if people of these two types try to negotiate, they may both feel frustrated by the other party's approach. The sales-oriented negotiator may become irritated by a perceived lack of interest, while the engineering-oriented negotiator may be frustrated by the lack of specifics. It's important to recognize these differences in behavioral style and to adjust your approach, if needed.

If you do find yourself reacting emotionally during the discussion, try to pause and take mental stock. What emotion are you feeling, and what is causing it? Are you feeling angry, upset, invigorated, excited? Is the other party intentionally pressing you to react emotionally? If so, why? Knowing that this is deliberate, and understanding the motivation, can help keep the negotiation balanced. If the emotional trigger is internal, and is caused by your own reaction to one of the issues under discussion, or to the other party, analyzing the reasons for the reaction can tell you a great deal about yourself—and can help you keep your cool.

Focus

Keep your sights on mutual gain, and on creating a win–win situation for both parties. Remember, the hiring process is not a hard-edged negotiation, but a collaborative one. Neither party should go away feeling shortchanged. In order to be successful in any negotiation, you need to understand both perspectives and motivations, the other party's and your own. Before you go into a discussion, define your objectives in terms of what you'd like to achieve. It can be helpful to prepare a written list. This gives you a framework, which will make you more comfortable trying to identify the other party's perspective. It will also help you refocus the discussion if it gets off track. Be an active listener, and ask questions to gain greater insight. Once you understand the other party's interests, it's easier to identify ways in which the interests of both sides can be met.

Four Key Areas of Negotiation

In their book, *Getting to YES,* Fisher, Ury, and Patton break negotiation down into four key areas:

1. Separate the people from the problem.
2. Focus on interests, not positions.
3. Invent options for mutual gain.
4. Insist on using objective criteria.

Each of these areas applies to the hiring process in two ways. First, these areas demonstrate to the interviewer your ability to communicate effectively and think on your feet—valuable skills on the job. And second, in combination, these four areas allow you to create a structured path through the hiring process and on to working successfully with others once you are hired.

Separate the People from the Problem

Many people involved in negotiations reach an impasse because they cannot separate the personal aspects of the negotiation from the actual problem they are trying to solve. Personal issues can arise on either side of the negotiation. These issues can involve people's perceptions, either of each other or of one of the issues being discussed. They can involve communication, either because one person doesn't present an issue clearly or because the other doesn't listen closely enough. Or they can involve emotions, on either side. In such situations, it's important to identify the real problem, and to separate personal feelings from the problem. Then, and only then, can you try to engage the other party, to figure out where he or she is coming from—and why.

> ***Example:*** As an independent consultant, Karen Silverman has worked with a lot of people in the publishing industry. Margery Goode, the editor in chief of Bookworks, recently called Karen to check on her availability for a new development they are looking into. The project sounds very interesting, and Karen is excited about the idea of working with Bookworks. However, her enthusiasm just suffered a major setback. A former co-worker left this message on her voice mail: "Karen, this is Lew Bauer. I'm now with Bookworks, and Marge told me that you'll be working with me on our new initiative. Give me a call, so we can set up a meeting to firm up your input, scheduling, pay scale, and so forth. I'm looking forward to working with you again."
>
> Lew may be looking forward to working with Karen, but the feeling isn't mutual. They last worked together three years ago, when both were in-house at the same publishing firm. Karen found Lew difficult to work with. He tended to be very controlling, and if other people didn't agree with him, he mocked and belittled them. When she left that job, she felt relieved that she would no longer need to work with Lew. Her first response to hearing his message is that she will have to say "no" to the Bookworks contract. Although the project will involve developing some highly desirable new skills, and the

Bookworks connection promises to be a lucrative one, she simply hates the idea of working with Lew again—and the thought of negotiating her contract with him is overwhelming.

Rather than making an impulsive decision based on emotion, Karen sat down and prepared a cost–benefit analysis of the situation. This helped her see that the biggest cost of accepting the project was a possible few months of a difficult work relationship, while the benefits included valuable new skills and a long-term connection with a new client. The benefits of turning the project down were limited to not having to work with Lew, while the costs would probably include a lasting regret at seeing someone else take an interesting, challenging new project. Since the benefits of taking the project far outweighed the costs, she called Lew to set up a meeting.

As she went in to the meeting, Karen reminded herself that she was able to set the parameters for their new working relationship. She focused on the questions that she needed to have answered, and refused to let her dislike of Lew affect the negotiation. To her surprise, Lew was also cordial and businesslike, and they quickly agreed to all the terms of the contract. In retrospect, Karen realized that Lew had just as much interest as she did in making sure the project worked—a concept she had forgotten when she was focusing on her unpleasant earlier association with him.

In the example above, Karen needed to identify the real problem, and to separate her personal feelings from the negotiation process. Her personal reaction to Lew was not relevant to the job. It also wasn't relevant to the negotiation process. By separating her personal feelings from her professional interests, Karen was able to successfully complete the negotiation.

Key Questions

Many negotiations are derailed by personality conflicts between the negotiating parties. Use questions like these to separate personal characteristics from the core problem:

- What is the real problem in this negotiation?
- What do I want to achieve in this negotiation?
- What does the other person want to achieve?
- How can I tell what he or she wants?
- Why might the other person take a certain position in the negotiation?
- What is my typical communication style (e.g., direct, tactful, outgoing, reserved)?
- What seems to be the other person's communication style?
- If there is a communication style mismatch, what can I do to bridge the communication gap?

Focus on Interests, Not Positions

We all bring two things with us to every negotiation: interests and positions. Our *interests* are the things we want to get from the negotiation. Our *positions* are the stances we take in order to achieve our interests. To negotiate successfully, it's important to focus on interests, not on positions. Why? Because positions are just the means to an end—a way to get our interests taken care of—but they can sometimes end up taking over the negotiation process. Once you take a position, it can be very hard to change. If you understand both your own interests and the other person's, you are in a better position to find a solution that meets both your needs.

> ***Example:*** Nina Clarke has applied for a job at Working World. They have made her an offer, and she is now meeting with Luke Arnold, the hiring manager. They've worked out most of the major areas of the employment agreement. However, they seem to have reached a real stumbling block on salary. From her research, Nina knows that this position should pay at least $90,000, but Luke has said firmly, "The company will offer you $80,000," and he refuses to budge on that figure. As Nina tries to figure out why Luke is so rigid on this, she realizes that Luke's wording has changed. On everything else they dis-

> cussed, Luke used phrases like "we can do this," or "I can offer you that." Now he's using "the company," not "I" or "we." Nina senses that the salary question is one Luke has no control over. Luke's rigid adherence to the salary he has named, combined with the types of challenges that were addressed in the interviewing process, lead Nina to suspect that the company is having cash-flow problems. Instead of pushing harder on the salary issue, Nina gets Luke involved in finding a solution. They negotiate a performance-based bonus schedule that will balance the company's salary offer with the compensation Nina knows she deserves. Months later, Nina learns that her hunch was right. Because of the company's cash-flow problems, the board had given Luke an absolute salary limit. By focusing on her interests—an appropriate overall compensation package—and not on the salary itself, Nina was able to negotiate for what she really needed despite the salary cap.

In this example, Nina and Luke opened the negotiation with a statement of their positions, not their interests. Only when Nina focused on the interests that lay behind their positions could a mutually agreeable solution be found. Nina's listening skills cued her in to Luke's tone change; she used a combination of intuition and deductive reasoning to identify the reasons for it. She was then able to conclude the negotiation successfully by using creative thinking to develop alternative solutions.

Identifying positions is fairly straightforward. However, uncovering the underlying interests is more challenging. People often start by stating their positions, without revealing the factors that led them to that position. A key approach to understanding the other party's interests is to ask questions in a nonthreatening manner.

Put yourself in the other person's shoes and ask, "Why are they taking that position? Why are they not making the decision I am asking them for?" If you still cannot determine why they are taking that position, you can—carefully—ask them why. When you do this, it is important to communicate the fact that you are trying to understand their concerns. If you take an empathic or understanding approach, you may get them to lower their barriers and talk about what's important to them. This will give you greater insight into their perspectives and interests, and will help you adjust your arguments to address their concerns.

In the example above, Nina asked herself several questions: *Why did Luke change his tone when talking about salary? Why can't he just offer me $10,000 per year more? Why did he change from saying "I" to saying "the company" when discussing salary?* The answer that best fit all these questions was "because increasing the salary is out of his control." Since this seemed a reasonable assumption, Nina realized that she needed to take another approach in order to have her needs met.

Key Questions

Everyone has interests in a negotiation. Positions lock you into a specific stance and can actually prevent compromise and agreement. Understand how to use your interests, and those of the other party, to achieve a successful negotiation. Ask yourself questions like these:

- What are my interests in this negotiation—what do I want to get out of it?
- How can I express my interests without taking a firm position that may be hard to change later?
- What are the other person's interests—what does he or she want to achieve?
- What leads me to believe these are his or her interests?
- Where do our interests connect or overlap?
- Why might the other person take a certain position in the negotiation?

Invent Options for Mutual Gain

Many people go into a negotiation thinking there is only one way to arrive at a positive outcome—only one "winning" solution. Unfortunately, each party may have a different "only" solution. Negotiations carried out with this approach can devolve into a win–lose situation: either I win and you lose, or you win and I lose. This type of negotiation is almost inevitably adversarial.

Instead of thinking of negotiation as the process of finding a *winning* solution, try thinking of it in terms of finding a *successful* solution. A successful solution is one that meets the interests of both parties.

You're much more likely to find a successful solution if you start the negotiations with an open mind. Think about the issue from both parties' perspectives, not just your own. What kinds of objections might the other party have to your solution—and why? Can you think of other ways to meet your interests that wouldn't raise the same objections?

> ***Example:*** Ray Gupta had accepted a job offer and was meeting with Arva Sloan, the hiring manager. Arva offered Ray an annual salary of $80,000, with a $5,000 signing bonus, plus stock options. Ray wanted a bonus of $10,000. However, Arva explained that the company had focused its capital on the upcoming product launch, which would make a $10,000 bonus at signing problematical. In Ray's response, he addressed Arva's concerns as well as his own. He pointed out that he was taking a slight salary cut, and that the stock options had no real value as yet. He acknowledged that the company needed to focus its cash on the product launch, but pointed out that there was still a lot of hard work ahead to make the product launch a success, and that his expertise would help make it successful. Then Ray made a counterproposal: a $5,000 bonus at signing, with another $5,000 to be paid over a ten-month period, in equal monthly installments of $500. Arva was able to balance the contributions Ray would make with his sensitivity to the company's cash-flow situation, and his willingness to be flexible. She agreed to his counterproposal.

In this example, the initial impediment could have brought the negotiations to a standstill. However, the candidate considered the positions and interests that both sides brought to the problem, and developed an option that addressed both parties' needs. By considering the hiring manager's perspective, and inventing a new option that satisfied both parties' interests, Ray was able to achieve his objective through negotiation.

Key Questions

There are many ways to resolve a dispute; looking at several different options increases the probability of a solution that both parties agree to. To facilitate this process, ask yourself questions like these:

- What is the fundamental problem in this negotiation?
- What are my interests and my solution?
- What are the other party's interests and solution?
- Where do our interests overlap?
- How does my solution conflict with the other party's interests?
- What other solutions might there be to the problem?
- What solutions address our mutual interests?

Insist on Using Objective Criteria

The basis for this method of negotiation is using objective criteria, not emotional ones. This means that your requests are reasonable, and you can refer to other sources to support those requests. A prospective employer won't agree to an astronomical salary because that's what you need to cover your expenses. Your personal budget is your business; the employer is more concerned with the company's budget—including the budget for salaries. To succeed in these negotiations, you need to be able to refer to credible third-party sources for information. You may not need to use those sources during the actual negotiation, but at least you'll be ready if you do need them.

Having objective criteria for your requests helps in other ways, too. If you don't have some objective basis for your requests, it's hard to go into a negotiation feeling confident—and it's easy to bend to pressure from the person you're negotiating with. If you base your requests on credible sources, you can approach the negotiation with confidence, and you can withstand pressure more easily because you know that what you're asking for is reasonable. You can also use the information to ground the discussion, by making reference to it from the start.

Example: Lori Anderson was interviewing for a position as senior controller at a medium-sized company, based in New York City, with annual revenues of $100 million. Alex Saunders, the hiring manager, made her an offer: $79,000, two weeks vacation, and benefits. Lori was interested in the position and the company; however, she was quite taken aback by the lowball offer. Alex explained that this was what the company had budgeted for this position, and they would very much like her to join the company. As part of her preparation for the negotiations, Lori had researched compensation for similar positions in the industry. Faced with a salary offer well below the range she expected, Lori initiated a discussion of salary levels at other New York–based companies of similar size and in the same industry. She asked Alex how the company had arrived at the compensation level, and solicited his opinion with regard to the Bureau of Labor Statistics as a source of information; Alex agreed that this was a reliable source. Once they had agreed on an objective source, Lori was able to show, to Alex's satisfaction, that the salary level for that position in the NYC region should actually be $90,000.

Because Lori had done her research, she did not feel pressure to take the lowball offer. And because she was able to introduce a mutually agreeable, objective source for salary information, she was able to establish fair standards for her compensation.

When using this method, it is important to be well prepared and to base your arguments firmly on the objective criteria. Armed with this knowledge, you will be ready to begin principled negotiation.

Key Questions

Objective criteria—criteria that are recognized as credible and impartial—ground your negotiation in reality and help legitimize your requests. Before going into the negotiation, be sure you have answers to questions such as these:

- What objective criteria are there for this situation (data for salaries, benefits, performance goals, etc.)?
- How do the objective criteria connect to my interests?

- Are the criteria acceptable to both parties?
- What variables can affect the criteria (location, company size, experience, etc.)?
- How can I use these criteria to support my interests?
- What other factors might reasonably affect the negotiation?

In the previous example, Lori came to the table with information that Alex did not have—Bureau of Labor Statistics figures for salaries in that industry and region. Some negotiators would have kept this information hidden, and tried to negotiate a salary higher than the industry standard. By being willing to share her information, Lori established a setting of openness and confidence for the negotiations.

This openness, and willingness to share information, is a key difference between principled negotiation and positional negotiation. In Lori's negotiation—and in all negotiations based on this process—there is no "winner" at the end of the negotiation, merely an agreement that both parties are satisfied with, and that both parties are likely to adhere to. Keep in mind the fact that this is the beginning of a long-term relationship between employer and employee, and you can lay the foundation for success in the long run.

The Three Stages of Negotiation

Most negotiations involve three stages: analysis, planning, and discussion. At the *analysis stage*, you evaluate the situation to see what the problem is, think about the problem, and organize the information you need to address the problem. At the *planning stage*, you generate options, prioritize the interests of both parties, set realistic objectives, and decide how you will approach the problem. At the *discussion stage*, you and the other party sit down to actually address the problem.

In most negotiations, we are unaware of these stages as separate ones; the whole negotiation process is often so quick that each stage lasts only a few moments. However, if we examine some of the negotiations used earlier as examples, we can see the three stages at work.

Our first example showed two friends trying to choose a restaurant. The analysis stage in this negotiation involved identifying the problem: both people wanted to eat, but one was firm in resisting Italian food. The planning stage involved prioritizing the interests of both parties—the person who wanted Italian food was willing to let the other person's interest prevail—and deciding what to do—have the other person suggest restaurants. The discussion stage involved generating options that would appeal to both parties—listing restaurants—and seeking agreement—choosing a restaurant that both would enjoy. The entire negotiation was probably just a few sentences long, but the three stages of negotiation were still present.

In the hiring process, the first two stages of the negotiation are done before you meet with the other person; they are part of your pre-negotiation preparation. In Part Two of this guide, we will address these three stages in the context of each element of the employment agreement, with specific questions you should be able to answer for each element.

Analysis

As in all negotiations, the first part of the process involves analyzing the overall situation. You need to understand the problem and organize the information required to address it. It's important to clearly define your objectives and the parameters surrounding your needs and wants. Determine your minimum requirements, your ideal, and your alternatives in the event that you can't negotiate a satisfactory agreement. Consider your own interests, and those of the other party, by doing a self-analysis and an opportunity analysis. In the Analysis section of each chapter in Part Two, we have provided a list of questions you should be able to answer for this stage of your preparation.

Planning

In negotiation, as elsewhere in life, preparation is the key. Before you sit down at the negotiating table, you need to do some research. Before interviewing, you researched the company. Did you learn anything new during the interview process that prompts you to look closely at a different aspect of the company? Or did you become aware of the need for more in-depth knowledge about a specific area? This is the time to fill in all the blanks.

As well as informing yourself about the company and the job, you will need to make sure you are well-informed about yourself—your strengths and your requirements. What do you want to gain from these negotiations with the company? Why do you want this?

You also need to look at the negotiation from the employer's point of view. Look at yourself as an investment the company is making. What would make you a successful investment? Prepare, as far as possible, for the employer's responses to your requests. Once you have outlined everything that would be in your ideal package, look at each element you've listed from the employer's point of view. Think of as many different reactions to each element as you can, from enthusiastic agreement to outraged refusal. You will be more effective—and more confident—if you are not surprised by the other party's responses.

In the Planning section of each chapter in Part Two, we have provided a list of questions you should be able to answer for this stage of your preparation.

Discussion

The third essential element in the negotiation process is the actual discussion. This is when both sides sit down together to work out the details of the agreement. As we look at each element in the employment agreement, we will address some of the specifics you will need to discuss, with suggestions of the types of questions you'll want to answer.

Every negotiation is different. It depends on the positions and interests both parties bring to the table, and on the individuals themselves—their personalities, their skills, and the way they respond to each other. Because there are so many variables, the process stage of every negotiation is also unique. You are the only one who can evaluate your own skills, interests, and attitudes, and those of the other party. For that reason, you can't follow a script to carry out the discussion stage of the negotiation.

However, there are certain questions you can ask to keep the discussion on track, and moving toward a successful conclusion. In the Discussion section of each chapter in this book, we have provided a list of questions that you might ask at each stage. These questions are designed to help you elicit the information you need in order to complete the negotiation. You might not ask all these questions in any one meeting. You might vary the order in which you ask them, and you will almost certainly vary the wording. But however you present them, these questions—and the answers they elicit—are the key to the discussion stage of the negotiation process.

Chapter Summary: Essentials of Negotiation

Four essential skills

- **Active listening.** Instead of using the other person's talk-time to work on your response, use it to really understand what is being said.
- **Clear communication.** Ask questions, interpret, and understand what is being said and why; then respond directly to the other person's statements.
- **Maintaining self-control and composure.** Remain consistent, separate personal feelings from the discussion, and don't react on an emotional level.
- **Focusing on the end goal.** Keep your sights on mutual gain and on creating a win–win situation for both parties.

Four key areas

- **Separate the people from the problem.** Avoid an impasse by separating personal aspects from the actual problem.
- **Focus on interests, not positions.** Understand your own interests as well as those of the other party, rather than just taking a stance and sticking to it.
- **Invent options for mutual gain.** Go in with an open mind; use creative thinking to reach an outcome that satisfies both parties' interests.

- **Insist on using objective criteria.** Use objective data, rather than emotional ones, to reinforce your arguments.

Three stages

- **Analysis.** Evaluate the situation to identify the problem, think about the problem, and organize the information to address the problem.
- **Planning.** Generate options, prioritize the interests of both parties, set realistic objectives, and decide how you will approach the problem.
- **Discussion.** Keep the negotiation on track and moving toward a successful conclusion by discussing the questions that address both parties' mutual interests.

CHAPTER TWO

Getting Ready to Negotiate

The first thing in any negotiation is listening, put on your ears and listen.
—Tom Wheeler, CEO, CTIA

There are three basic ways to get a new job: (1) through a *third-party referral* where someone you know suggests you as a candidate, based on their knowledge of and belief in your abilities; (2) through a *professional recruiting firm,* where a recruiter identifies and solicits you; or (3) through a *blind venue*—a job posting on an on-line career site, a classified advertisement, or other media.

Each of these ways of finding a job is viable; however, each creates a different perception in the mind of your future employer. Why is this important? Each has a different initial impact on your ability to negotiate. It is very possible that a candidate coming through any of these avenues can negotiate the same deal, but the best possible route is through a third-party referral where you are currently employed and a trusted source has already started to build your value in the eyes of the hiring manager.

A retained recruiter who solicits you while you are employed elsewhere is also an excellent way to pave the way to successful negotiations. However, because the employer is paying the recruiter—usually one-third of your base salary—there are conflicting interests. The recruiter wants to get you the best salary possible, but he or she is really working for the company, and the company is sensitive to expensive recruiting costs. Although you are building a relationship with the recruiter, you should remember who is paying the fee; however, a good recruiter will be genuine in his or her intention to help identify the right match for both the company and you.

An on-line job posting, classified advertisement, or other blind venue is the third way of securing a job. This has both advantages and drawbacks. The advantage is that if you make a favorable impression on the company you can negotiate a better deal because the company does not have to pay expensive recruiting costs. The drawbacks are that the screening process is less informed, since the candidate does not know as many details as through the other venues; there are more candidates to compete with because it is indirect job solicitation; and often you do not have as much control over the whole process.

All three of these approaches can result in your entering into the interviewing and negotiating process, but the amount of leverage you have in the process varies from one to another. As a general rule, if you approach the company as the result of a blind venue, you have the least leverage in the negotiations; if the company initiates the contact and seeks to recruit you, you have the most leverage. While the impression you make on the interviewer can offset this to a degree, you should keep this in mind as you approach your negotiation.

◆ Preparation

With any challenge in life, the better prepared you are to meet the challenge, the more successful you'll be in tackling it. Whether it's training for a marathon or studying for an exam, the greater your familiarity with a routine or subject, the more adept you'll be in navigating your way through it. A negotiation is no different.

By clearly defining your interests and anticipating those of the other party, you will increase your effectiveness in any negotiation. For the purposes of this guide, we focus on principled negotiations. Principled negotiations are not about winning and losing, but about reaching an outcome where both parties' interests are satisfied through a constructive discussion process. In order to engage in such a discussion, you need to understand your objectives and to enter the discussion with a mind open to the other party's perspectives. The more you can learn about the other party's ethics, values, and personal attributes, and about the company, the greater your negotiating effectiveness; you'll have a better understanding of the other person, which will give you an increased level of comfort in your discussions.

Before any negotiation discussion, think of yourself as a private investigator. It's your job to research, gather clues, gain insights, and make deductions based on information about the organization. Therefore, your focus should be on thorough preparation, with the goal of minimizing surprises and maximizing the degree to which you can anticipate the other party's responses. We've highlighted the three key areas of preparation that will help you get ready for any career negotiation discussion. We addressed not only the areas that relate to the discovery and research process about the company, the job's duties, the people you'll be working for and with, but also ways to increase your leverage and perceived value in the eyes of the other party. If you follow these steps, they will provide you with a structured framework from which you can begin to build a solid platform for any negotiation.

Identify Your Needs, and the Company's

The first step in any negotiation is to do thorough research before the negotiation actually begins. You need to define what you want, determine what the employer will be willing and able to offer, and calculate the compensation range that's appropriate for the job you'll be filling. The more you know going into the negotiation—about yourself, the employer, the industry, and the issues that concern the employer—the better off you'll be. It's important to try to learn as much as possible about the other party's background and the organization, and to try to envision, before the interview, what the other's thinking might be and what contributions you can make to effect positive change within the organization.

There are many resources you can use to find the answers to these questions. As well as searching the Web, try to find out everything you can on a company through books, publications, and networking with contacts to gain insight from an insider's perspective. You must first rely on your own analytical skills to identify the areas that are important to you. Then, from discussions with individuals within the company and throughout the interview process, it's important to gauge the employer's perspective and to learn as much as possible about the company, its culture, and the general philosophies of the people you will be working with. These techniques help give you an overall "feel" for the company and its people. However, it's also important to locate objective data about salary levels, geographic location, size of company, and industry.

Once you've gathered the data you can perform an objective analysis of an offer. By relying on and presenting objective, credible data, you'll have greater leverage in your negotiation because neither party can argue the facts. Therefore, think carefully about your overall objectives, and clearly define both your ideal package and what you would be willing to accept. By defining these scenarios in advance, you will be more at ease during the discussion process because you'll have already considered multiple options. This will enable you to be more decisive and clear in your communication because the parameters are clearly defined in your mind.

Once you have a clear game plan and approach, your next challenge is to build your value in the employer's eyes—to show why you are a worthwhile investment for the company. Identify your core strengths, unique skills, and background, and be prepared to explain to the interviewer how your experience will benefit the company. Many interviewees find it helpful to prepare a script in advance for this part of the interview, and to practice presenting it; this will help you appear at ease and confident during the interview.

All your advance work will prepare you for the most challenging aspect of the negotiation: the actual discussion. Negotiations can take various twists and turns. It's important to think on your feet, but remember to stick to your game plan and adapt where appropriate. Also, avoid arguments that are focused around your personal needs. Although your needs are important to you, they are not relevant to your discussion with the interviewer. Structure the discussion of your needs in terms of benefit to the company. For example, if you need $4,000 more per year to cover daycare, you might reposition your argument thus: "I plan to work as many hours as the position requires and want my mind to be 100 percent focused on my job. However, I want to ensure that my personal security obligations are sufficiently met." Always keep in mind how your points will come across from the company's perspective. By appealing to their interests, you will increase your chances for reaching agreement.

Key Questions

Before going into a negotiation, be sure you know what you want to achieve, and what the company wants to achieve.

- What are your overall objectives?
- What do you want?
- What do you need?
- What's your bottom line?
- What are the other party's driving motivations?
- What are their interests?

Identify the Details

The second step in the negotiating process involves creating a detailed negotiation plan for yourself and writing out an agenda describing the details that have to be worked out. You might want to create a concrete list of what's important to you, from the details of your job description to compensation-related issues such as salary, benefits, bonus, severance, etc. Your objective in doing the preparation should be to anticipate everything that could possibly happen during the negotiation, and what the employer's needs and desires are. Be prepared to handle any situation. By creating a specific and well-defined plan, you will enhance your ability to stay on topic, maintain clear communications, and address your objectives. It's also useful to prioritize the issues that are most important to you so that you can first address those that are highest on the list, then move to the lesser issues. Just because you made a list of ten issues, you don't have to negotiate on each; choose the issues that are most important to you, and focus on those areas.

Key Questions

Establish a negotiation plan, including options to pursue and details to resolve.

- What options support your interests?
- What objective criteria (salary data, established performance goals, etc.) can you use in the negotiation?
- How might the employer react to your proposals? How will you respond?
- What is your plan for the negotiation?
- What issues are most important to you, and what are you willing to compromise on?
- How can you communicate your interests in a way the other person will understand?
- What will you do to establish rapport with the other person?

Identify Your Alternatives

You've decided that this job is a great match for your skills, the location is ideal, and the work environment is exactly what you've been looking for. The best option for you is to get this job, with the ideal compensation package you've already worked out. We'll call this Job #1. What's your second-best option? What's your BATNA—your Best Alternative to a Negotiated Agreement?

Developing a clear BATNA is an essential step in the negotiations process. Essentially, the BATNA is your fallback position: "If I don't get this job, then I'll . . . ". Having a well thought out BATNA will help you at every step of the hiring process.

Knowing your BATNA means you can negotiate for the job you really want with confidence. Usually, a job negotiation involves a lot of uncertainty: What if this doesn't work out? Am I really the best person for this job? What is a reasonable salary and benefits package for this job? How can I tell if they're making a reasonable offer? Identifying your BATNA helps to eliminate much of this uncertainty. If this negotiation doesn't work out, then you'll go with your BATNA. And if your BATNA is another job, then you'll already know whether the offer a company is making you is a reasonable one. Having a clear BATNA lets you really compare job offers.

Let's say you're currently working in middle management in a large firm and you're interviewing for an upper-management job in a small firm in another city—say, Cleveland. Comparing your current job and the new job is like comparing apples and pineapples—they're completely different things.

Take a good look at all your options. Do the same kind of analysis and preparation as you did for the job you really want. Is your current job your only alternative if the job in Cleveland doesn't work out? Is there another, almost equally attractive, job opening in Tucson? Or would this be the time for you to follow up on that idea you had for starting your own business? Which of the other options is the best alternative? If you can't negotiate a satisfactory agreement for the job in Cleveland—your Job #1— what's the next best *realistic* choice? Maybe you have a business idea but no experience in the area you want to start the business in, and no financing. You would need to do a lot more preparation before starting that business would be a realistic choice. That would make either your current job or the job in Tucson—Job #2—your fallback position, your best alternative, your BATNA.

To make sure you really do have a concrete BATNA, you should complete the negotiations process for Job #2 before you negotiate for Job #1. Why? Because then you'll know exactly what your second-best option is—the option you'll take if Job #1 doesn't work out. You'll be able to compare any offers Job #1 makes you to a comparable job instead of a very different one. If Job #1 offers you a salary of $85,000 and Job #2 had offered you $80,000, you can analyze the reasonableness of this salary. On the other hand, if Job #2 offered you $120,000 and Job #1 is only willing to offer you $75,000, you have a good reason to ask questions.

A second advantage to having a firm BATNA before going into negotiations is that you can negotiate from a position of strength. Instead of negotiating with a "Job #1 or bust" attitude, you can negotiate knowing that you already have a very attractive alternative waiting in the wings. You're less likely to accept an employer's opening offer when you've already been offered something much better elsewhere.

Also, the security of having a clear BATNA enables you to present a confident demeanor during the negotiations. It's a great morale booster. It's much easier to appear confident when you don't feel that everything is riding on this one agreement. (See the Executive's Insight section in the chapter on salary for an example of the BATNA at work.)

Clarifying your BATNA before starting negotiations also helps make you clear about concrete options, not options in the aggregate. Perhaps, on entering the negotiations for Job #1, you might find yourself thinking, "Well, if this doesn't work out, I could always start my own business, or take Job #2, or I could just stay at my current job." It's important not to look at your alternatives in the aggregate—Job #2 + own business + current job. These three combined probably have more advantages than Job #1. Remember that you can't take all three options—you have to choose one. If you take Job #2, you can't also stay in your current job; if you start your own company, you can't take Job #2. Developing a clear BATNA in advance helps you avoid this kind of aggregate thinking, so you really do compare only your top two options—the job you are interviewing for and your BATNA, whatever that may be.

Key Questions

Develop your BATNA (Best Alternative to a Negotiated Agreement). Use it to give you confidence and, if necessary, for negotiating leverage.

- What is your Job #1?
- What are your alternatives? List at least three; be reasonable and specific.
- What does each opportunity offer (pros and cons)?

Chapter Summary: Getting Ready to Negotiate

- **Define your interests and anticipate those of the other party.** Clearly identify your objectives and prepare in advance to address the other person's needs.

- **Identify your needs, and the company's.** Do thorough research, understand your needs, and the needs of the company. Determine your bottom line, your ideal, and your acceptable range; the area of flexibility in the negotiations is between what you need and what you want. If you get less than you need, the negotiation process has not been successful.
- **Build your value proposition.** Think through in advance what you bring to the table, including skills and specific accomplishments. The company is making an investment in you; you must convince them that you are a viable investment.
- **Avoid bringing personal needs into the discussion.** Rather than discussing your personal needs, position the discussion in terms of the company's needs. Present your personal needs as a benefit for the company.
- **Identify the details.** Create a detailed negotiation plan for yourself and write out an agenda describing the issues that need to be addressed. A well-defined plan will enhance your ability to stay on topic.
- **Identify your alternatives.** Develop a clear BATNA (Best Alternative to a Negotiated Agreement) as your fallback position.
- **Anticipate the employer's objections.** Before the negotiation, think about how the employer is likely to respond to your request, and be prepared to respond to objections. Focus on emphasizing your value to the company, using specific accomplishments to reinforce this.
- **Make your discussion a win–win process.** Avoid confrontation. It's not wise to negotiate hard on everything; choose the issues that are most important to you. Keep in mind that you hope to work with the other party, and you're trying to build a relationship, not score points.
- **Be creative and agile.** As the saying goes, "If at first you don't succeed, try again." There are many ways to arrive at a mutually beneficial solution. Be prepared to pro-

pose and discuss alternative options that address both parties' interests.

- **Be prepared to walk away.** Based on your determination of what you need, you have to be willing to walk away if you don't get it. If you're not willing to walk away, you are at a disadvantage from the start.

PART TWO

The Negotiations Begin

CHAPTER THREE

The Interview

You can analyze the situation, but the key is analyzing the person, the personality.
—Bob Welsh, AFL-CIO

◆ The Challenge and Overview

The hiring process is a multistep negotiation where the needs of both parties are clearly defined: The company needs to fill a position and you need to secure a job. The process also involves building a relationship and mutual confidence with the other party, which does not happen in just one interview. Confidence requires trust; it's important, if you make a commitment—however small—to keep it. Let's say you're planning on following up after your interview because the company asked for additional information; a prompt response to the request is an excellent way to build confidence immediately.

There are other small signs that indicate to each party that there may be a good fit—or not. Your ability to communicate effectively, to listen, think, and respond, will help you successfully build a relationship with the other party. The more engaging and revealing you are, the greater the interest you will generate in the interviewer.

The biggest potential obstacle here is if the employer hasn't defined what they're looking for. If they don't know what they want, you can't convince them that you meet their needs. On the flip side, some interviewees set themselves up for failure at this point by exaggerating their skills in an area to get the job. Doing this practically guarantees that you won't succeed on the job.

Essentially, the interview is your opportunity to understand the problem the employer is experiencing and to articulate the ways in which your skills, experience, and work style will contribute to resolving that problem. The problem can be on an organizational level or a departmental level; it may be as simple as needing to replace an excellent employee who has been promoted, or it may involve operational difficulties. Simple or complex, resolving this problem is the foundation of the company's interest in the negotiation. Your challenge is to convince the interviewer that hiring you will solve the problem. This is their interest. Resolving this challenge is their goal for hiring someone; addressing their interests early on in the interview will make sure you position yourself strategically for the job. Therefore, as Tom Wheeler, CEO of the Cellular Telecommunications Industry Association, advises, "Put on your ears and listen." Active listening will help you quickly grasp the other party's interests. You can then respond to their needs with specific examples of how your skills and experience will positively address the hiring manager's needs and those of the company.

◆ Preparation

The interview stage is the most important part of the job-seeking process; this is the point at which you first present yourself and gain some understanding of the other party. You're trying to make a good impression and present yourself in the best light, while at the same time learning as much as you can about the other person. As the company is determining whether you are the right candidate, you must do the same type of analysis. The company must analyze whether you are worth investing in; any human capital resource expenditure must be looked at by the company in terms of its return on investment for paying you $100,000 or more. You must do the same analysis and make the same determination: Will working at this company give you a long-term return in terms of career migration path, quality of life, and the opportunity to learn and work with others in a stimulating environment?

As an executive, it's not just about money. The number one

reason people stay at companies is the environment and the people they work with. Money is the easiest area to figure out. Other areas take much more time, and are often the most critical. Just as the company has prepared interview questions, so should you. If one of their hires does not work out, the impact on the company is not nearly as great as the impact on you if you end up leaving because of a mismatch.

In order to identify whether the work environment and career path opportunities are a good fit, you need to do some advance work, such as researching the company via printed and on-line resources and accessing your network of colleagues and friends, who might provide greater insight into the company's culture, business philosophies, and overall health. Once you've gathered this information, you may find yourself more positive about the opportunity, or you may find that you need to probe further.

Another valuable effect of preparation is that it enables you to plan how to position your skills and experience during the interview. As you research the company, look for specifics that you can tie in to your background—for example, how your industry contacts or sales-channel knowledge will add value to the sales and marketing area, or how your engineering training and experience on previous development projects will augment their current teams.

Once you have prepared the key points that you want to address, you will be more focused and confident during the interview process because you'll have defined goals of what you want to achieve.

A less discussed but important component of the preparation process is being ready to observe and interpret the interviewer's body language. First, it's helpful to understand the parameters of your interview, for example, the time allotted, whom you will be meeting with, and their backgrounds. Once you've gathered this information and are engaged in the interview, you can gauge your connection through direct or indirect eye contact. Does the interviewer constantly look at her watch or glance at her computer screen? Does he fidget in his chair, or shuffle papers? Is this the interviewer's personal style, or do you need to do something to re-engage his or her attention? An effective tactic to re-engage a distracted interviewer is to ask a question that relates either to something he or she said or to an area that is in line with your investigative research. This approach draws the interviewer's attention back to the discussion. If you fail to draw the interviewer's full attention back to your discussion, this might be indicative of his or her personality, or it might indicate that there is a disconnection, which you must take into consideration after the interview.

◆ The Negotiation

During the interview process, you are trying to present yourself in the best possible light, to find out as much as you can about the company, and to determine whether the job is a good fit for your skills, experience, interests, and personality—all at the same time! Here are some of the key questions that will help you assess how good a match you and the company will be. In the analysis and planning stages, ask yourself the relevant questions. In the discussion stage, use these questions as a basis for your discussion with the interviewer.

Analysis

Analyze the situation, your interests, and those of the other party, and begin gathering information. Consider your own interests, and those of the other party, by doing a self-analysis and an opportunity analysis. You will need to develop answers to questions like these:

Key Questions

Self-Analysis

- What is my ideal job?
- What are my criteria for making a job decision?
- What work environment is ideal for my behavioral type?
- How willing am I to adapt to a work environment that is different from my ideal?
- What do I want to get from this opportunity?
- What do I have to offer this employer?
- How do my skills, experience, and strengths relate to the job requirements?

Opportunity Analysis

- What data can I collect about the company (e.g., size, geographic location, financial performance, values/mission, leadership team, product lines/markets served)?
- What does my analysis of the data tell me about the company's financial health, culture, philosophy, and expectations?
- What is the work environment like?
- What is the employer looking for?
- Where does the position fit within the organization?
- What is the manager's communication style? How can I "read" the interviewer and communicate in the manner he/she prefers?

Planning

Use planning to establish your strategy, understand the other party's interests, and determine what options or alternatives would be acceptable outcomes.

Key Questions

- What does the employer want? (Consider job advertisements and position descriptions, as well as what the employer tells you when scheduling the interview.)
- What are the interests of the employer and the hiring manager?
- What problem is the employer trying to solve by filling this position? What can I do to solve the problem?
- What is my second-best job opportunity (BATNA)?
- Is my BATNA a concrete offer, or is it still in the early stages of discussion?

Discussion

During the negotiation, you can collect new information in two ways: through questions you ask the interviewer, and through unsolicited information the interviewer shares as part of the discussion. These are some of the questions you should ask and information you should listen for.

Questions to Ask

- What skills are you looking for, ideally?
- What are the company's short-term goals (3–6 months)?
- What are the company's longer-term goals (12–18 months)?
- What makes the company unique? How would you distinguish it from your competitors?
- What is the financial condition of the company? What are its funding sources (relevant for small, privately held companies or non-profits that rely on grants for their funding)?
- Can you talk about the management team? What are their management philosophies?
- What is the intracompany environment like—from a social/team-building perspective? What was the last time there was a company social event?
- With whom would I be working?
- What would be the first projects I would work on?
- What is the decision-making process within this department? Within the company as a whole?
- Does the company offer any noncompensation benefits (telecommuting, health club, flex-time)?
- What does the company do to demonstrate its commitment to investing in people/professional development?
- How would you describe the work environment?
- Get permission to talk to other employees by saying, "Can I talk with a few potential colleagues about their perspectives on the company?" Then ask employees questions such as:
  —Can you describe the company's environment?
  —What is it like to work for [the interviewer or the person you'll be working for]?

—What do you like best about working at the company?
—Is there anything that has frustrated you during your employment?
—How do company leaders demonstrate commitment to the company's values or mission (e.g., customer service, innovation, growth targets, etc.)?

Information to Listen For

- Problems the employer hopes to solve by filling the vacant position
- Financial condition of the organization (may be indicated by reluctance to share financial information or future plans)
- Benefits offered, including health insurance, retirement contributions, time off, and work/life initiatives
- Work environment and corporate culture (e.g., collaborative teamwork, social events, enthusiasm, hours worked)

◆ Outcome: Next Steps

After the interview, outcomes can vary depending on the size and processes of the company. It's important to gauge the other party's thoughts, not necessarily by asking, but by saying something like,"I've enjoyed the time we spent together today, so I am curious as to the next steps of the process." You may get a favorable and reaffirming response, such as, "I enjoyed it too, and there are a couple of other people I would like you to talk with." This indicates that you've made a positive impression, and the company is interested in pursuing the process. You may also receive a more ambiguous response, such as, "Well, we're interviewing a lot of candidates and we'll get back to you once the process is complete." If you get an ambiguous response, it's always reasonable to ask about the hiring time frame. You may also want to ask whether there is any other information they need from you.

Immediately after your interview, it's important to send a follow-up e-mail or note, thanking them for their time, reaffirming your interest in the company and position, and possibly including a brief reference to an interesting area of discussion explored in your interview. The whole job-seeking process is essentially about relationship building; therefore, any appropriate and warm human touch that conveys your thoughtfulness and unique style will help to distinguish you in the eyes of the interviewer.

Executive's Insight: The Interview

R. D. Whitney is vice president of operations with a leading professional services information provider. In this section, he discusses his experience with the interview process. The win–win principles exemplified in this excerpt are shown in the right-hand margin of the text.

"My previous position was production manager for the North American operations of a Dutch publishing company—a large, structured organization. Before that, I was production manager at a U.S.–based publishing company. I wanted get into something a bit different, a more entrepreneurial company. It was through networking that I met the man who had recently purchased this company.

Principles in Action: Identify your needs.

"The company had been a family organization, and the new CEO was starting to grow the company, so he was looking to hire some staff. I met him through a colleague, heard what he had in mind for the company, and decided that this was the opportunity I was looking for. I told him about my experience, how I could contribute to the organization, and we found that it was a good match.

Principles in Action: Identify the company's needs.

"To prepare for that initial interaction with the CEO, I tried to learn as much as I could about his background and the organization, and tried to envision, before the interview, where he was thinking of taking the organization, what possibilities existed for a business that had been around for thirty years but was about to undergo a major change. So as well as the obvious, researching the

Principles in Action: Research the company.

company, looking on the Web, I went to a library, found the company's books and publications, things like that.

"Looking at the existing products showed me the potential for the company. It needed to repackage and reposition the current products, and do some new product development based on core assets, but I could see that there were some real gems here.

Principles in Action: Identify the problems you can solve for the employer.

"When the CEO and I first met, the first step—as in a lot of interviews—was selling from both sides. He was selling the organization and its potential, and I was selling my skills and background and how I could increase and develop that potential. It also involved us getting to know each other a bit to see if we shared similar beliefs and values. You know, your work is one of the biggest investments in time you can make, and you can choose where to work or who to work for, so that kind of assessment is an important part of your thought processes.

Principles in Action: Build your value proposition.

"The next step was getting to know the organization a little better. I already knew some of the people in the organization, but I needed to see the team that was forming, to learn a bit about their experience and backgrounds, ambitions and goals. I also needed to learn more about the company objectives, whether they were reachable, or if they were conservative. All in all, we had a total of three meetings, during the course of which I met with at least 80 percent of the organization, and spoke with the other 20 percent.

Principles in Action: Speak to current employees to learn about the company.

"The biggest challenge of the whole process was that I had a short time to try to understand the organization and the people in it, and to decide whether this was a place where I wanted to spend a great deal of my life—while at the same time trying to sell myself to the organization, and to present my experience and philosophy in an interesting light. To achieve that part of my goals, I pointed to my experience, my past accomplishments. I gave detailed examples of myself as a manager, of how I've handled situations.

"I think the process of job negotiations starts as soon as you make contact. Both sides have to set expectations, and a lot of selling goes on between both sides. Then, as both sides get to know each other a bit, you start to frame the references of what could potentially be an employment situation. There are certain things that both sides can and can't accept.

Principles in Action: The negotiation begins with the interview.

"To ensure success in the interview, you need to start way before the first interview, getting to know the company. Some of it will be through investigative work, and some through networking. If you don't understand the opportunity, you're going in there blind; you have no idea if you are a match or what the potential really is. It's a lot like selling a product. You should know your customer when you walk in to make a sale, and you should have an idea in your head of what you are willing to sell the product for. The customer will have an idea of what they're willing to pay, but if you're a good salesperson, you can enhance the value of your product by showing the benefits rather than the features. You can show the customer how that product is going to help. In the case of the interview, you show the interviewer that hiring you will help make more money or will help grow the organization.

Principles in Action: Identify the details.

"In terms of salary, you want to do whatever research you can, and at least form a range that would be acceptable to you and the scenario that would be acceptable to you. The employer is going to have a range in mind, too. In the interviewing process, you each get to know the other's range and limits as each meeting goes on. You do as much as you possibly can before each meeting, and there comes a point where the employer and potential employee both say, 'OK, let's show our cards,' and that's the point where your research can end; you have a good idea of where the range is, and if it's something that you're realistically going to be able to achieve.

Principles in Action: Use objective criteria.

"An important thing to remember in the job negotiations process is that the people involved in the hiring are very, very busy. Although you're an important part of what they are trying to accomplish, they also have business to conduct. Don't get nervous if you haven't heard from them for a while, but stay on top of it. It's like following up on any sale—don't be hesitant about following up, making some personal contact, maybe an e-mail just to see how things are going. You'll get a good sense of where you stand. In my case, the CEO had a very personal involvement throughout the hiring process. He kept me informed, and then there was a formal phone call and a formal written offer.

"At that point, I did very little more negotiating. There were a couple of things I pushed for, and they were met. But this is not the point where you can say, oh, the salary is off by 30 percent. It's a point where you can go for some minor concessions if they were vague in the interviewing process. Yes, there is an opportunity here, but you should use it very, very sparingly. Don't use it as a way to push for more. If something is particularly important to you, you can make the case at that point, but there's always the risk that you'll win the battle but lose the war. This is the point where the sales technique stops and you become one of them. So look in their eyes, and think about what is in the best interests of the company, but don't push too hard.

Principles in Action: Focus on building a long-term relationship.

"One of the most important things to remember in the job search process is, life is short. You don't have to accept any position; don't get steered into a position you don't want to accept. There's a lot of opportunity out there. If you're a talented, energetic person, you'll have lots of options; don't settle. Look for your dream job. You're going to be spending most of your life there, so be passionate about what you're going to do. That's my biggest piece of advice."

Chapter Summary: The Interview

- **The negotiation begins with your interview.** Use it to build the relationship and mutual confidence.
- **Do your homework.** Research the company, environment, and position thoroughly.
- **Build your value proposition in advance.** Be prepared to discuss your skills, achievements, and experience.

- **Ask investigative questions.** Understand what the employer wants, what problems you can solve, why your skills and experience make you the ideal candidate, and why the organization is the right place for you.
- **Be an active listener.** Distinguish the organization's interests from the hiring manager's interests. Understand how the position fits into the organization and why it is important.
- **Convince them that you meet their needs.** Use your knowledge of the employer's needs and interests to express how your background will benefit the company.
- **Always have your second-best job alternative in hand.** Know your BATNA (best alternative to a negotiated agreement) so you'll have greater confidence that an acceptable alternative exists.

CHAPTER FOUR

Salary

Raising the subject of money is hard for some people. But once you start doing it, you learn to get better at it.

—Cale Graham
VP, Strategic Planning

◆ The Challenge and Overview

Almost everyone negotiates this area of the employment agreement, but for many people, the topic is an uncomfortable one. Also, salary is typically only one part of the overall compensation package. While the different elements of the package are often negotiated separately, it is important to look at the package as a whole.

To determine an appropriate salary range, you need to examine four key variables: *company size, industry, geographic location,* and *comparable positions.* The importance of most of these variables is self-evident, but some candidates overlook the importance of company size. Obviously, larger companies have greater financial resources in terms of salaries. However, they also often have rigid salary budgets. Also, when negotiating with a large company, you are less likely to be in direct contact with members of senior management—the individuals with the authority to authorize a salary that is higher than the company standard, or a stronger stock options, bonus, and benefits package.

As well as evaluating outside factors, you need to analyze your own financial needs. What salary do you want to earn? What do you need to meet your financial obligations? What would you be willing to accept?

Then, in the actual interview, you need to integrate your needs and those of the company, and to make sure they are balanced. If your needs are not in tune with those of the company, then you will not be able to reach a mutually agreeable outcome.

◆ Preparation

The salary is typically the first component of any job offer that is addressed. Prepare for this step by gathering as much factual and objective information as you can. These are the most important pieces of information you must collect, using your own resources, research, your network contacts, and/or your recruiter. To research comparable salaries, industry associations and Internet-based salary calculators are good starting points. Then, make sure to take all these variables into account:

- ***Similar positions within your industry.*** If you are interviewing for a COO position in the telecom industry, you must not look at similar positions in software.
- ***Cost-of-living comparisons.*** If you are looking to relocate from Phoenix, AZ to New York City, the cost of living will be much higher in NYC; you must further refine your research to include COO positions in the telecom industry in the NYC metro area.
- ***Company size.*** Many Internet-based salary calculators do not take company size into consideration when calculating commensurate executive pay; they usually just provide position, industry, and region-based pay. This can skew the salary range, because smaller companies often cannot afford the large executive salary that medium-to-large companies offer. Also, smaller companies often have a more aggressive stock option compensation plan, which must be considered part of the overall compensation package.

There are many sources for this information, from print and Internet resources (such as *The Wall Street Journal; National Business Employment Weekly; Working Woman* magazine, which publishes an annual salary survey; www.salaryexpert.com, provided by Baker, Thomsen Associates, a compensation and benefits consulting firm) to professional associations or colleagues or friends in the industry. Although friends and colleagues can provide useful anecdotal information, to establish a credible basis for salary negotiation, it's important to identify objective criteria.

Once you've collected and compiled this information, you can build a framework for solid salary negotiations. If an employer makes you an offer that is low compared to the figures you have collected, you will be able to build a strong case based on published salary data for the industry.

If you believe in your ability to deliver, you may be able to structure a salary based on achieving milestones. If this is the case, it is important to be specific and outline these points in your offer letter so there is no ambiguity (i.e., describe the milestones or objectives in a concrete or tangible format, like gross sales number or product development milestones, then what specific compensation you should receive in the event that you achieve those objectives).

◆ The Negotiation

Negotiating salary is a common, but complex, challenge. It's critical that you look carefully at your compensation requirements before the discussion phase because you only get one real shot to set the bar or respond to the first offer. Therefore, do your research, identify objective criteria in terms of commensurate salary levels in similar industries, and be able to clearly articulate why you are worth what you are asking for.

Once you're in the discussion phase, you can explore related compensation topics such as bonuses and stock options. The preparation that you make before this discussion will also help you in related discussions and will let you know your limitations as they arise. The questions below will help you prepare for this phase.

Analysis

Analyze the situation, your interests, and those of the other party, and begin gathering information. Consider your own interests, and those of the other party, by doing a self-analysis and an opportunity analysis. You will need to develop answers to questions like these:

Key Questions

Self-Analysis

- What is my salary range?
- What is the minimum I could earn to support myself?
- What is my "pie-in-the-sky" figure?
- Is it important to me to have all my compensation be salary-based, or am I willing to have some income based on commission?
- What salary, somewhere between the minimum and maximum ranges, is a figure I'd be happy with?
- What do people in similar positions in my industry/ profession earn?

Opportunity Analysis

- How big is the company?
- Where is it located?
- Are there objective salary data specific to this type of organization?
- If the compensation includes commission, is it based on net revenue or gross revenue?
- How critical to the company's success is the role I am pursuing?
- How long has the position been vacant? How long has the organization been searching for someone to fill the position?

Planning

Use planning to establish your strategy, understand the other party's interests, and determine what options or alternatives would be acceptable outcomes. Ask yourself questions like these as part of your planning process:

Key Questions

- What salary does my BATNA offer?
- How will I redirect questions about my desired salary level?
- Do I have objective criteria to support a particular salary?
- Does the person I'm meeting with have the authority to make salary decisions?
- What salary constraints might the company have (e.g., salary grades, HR oversight, tight cash flow)?
- What other options might help me realize the overall compensation package I need?

Discussion

These are some of the questions you should ask during the negotiation. These questions should only be asked after a formal offer has been made. Avoid putting the first salary figure on the table. You should always wait for the company to make the first offer. If asked what you're looking for, it is safe to respond first with a statement like, "I will consider any reasonable offer." If that fails, turn the question back to the other person by saying, "You're in a better position to know how much I'm worth to you than I am."

Questions to Ask

- What is the actual salary being offered?
- How was that figure determined?
- How often is salary reviewed?
- What is the salary review process?
- What are the salary review measurement criteria?
- Can salary reviews be scheduled more frequently than once a year—say, every three months, or every six months?
- What performance expectations must be met to earn a raise or move into the next salary grade?

- If the company is not open to salary negotiations, is it open to performance-based bonuses, commission, stock options, or additional benefits to augment salary?

◆ Outcome: Next Steps

Once you have completed the negotiations, it is important to get a clear understanding of the terms you negotiated. It is valuable to reiterate all the terms that relate to salary. This may include a signing bonus and/or performance bonus, both of which are described in detail in Chapter Six. The next step is to ask the employer when you can expect an employment agreement that will specifically outline the salary terms.

Illustrated below is salary language from an executive's employment agreement. Important aspects include:

- ***Commencement Date.*** Make sure that there is a clear start date so that, if you are resigning from your current job, you are protected. This will legally bind your future employer to this salary commitment.
- ***Annual Salary.*** Your annualized salary should be explicitly stated, and there should be provisions for standard annual increases to adjust for normal cost of living and inflation.
- ***Payment Terms.*** It is wise to have the frequency of payroll stated clearly so that you can plan your personal cash flow needs accordingly. If you also negotiated a sales commission or gross revenue overrides, it is not uncommon to see the salary disbursement on a biweekly basis and the sales commissions on a monthly or quarterly basis; this should all be clearly stated.
- ***Compensation Caps.*** In smaller companies, executive salaries may include salary caps because total sales are lower than in large companies and companies want to ensure that no one employee has too high a percentage of overall revenue. In addition, executives often have significant stock options; once they reach a certain salary level, they want to have the additional cash resources to invest in growing the company and increasing their

stock value. If you have a salary cap, ensure that the fiscal year(s) are accurately stated, clarifying the month and fiscal year end.

Example as Excerpted from an Executive's Employment Agreement

3.1 Salary. Commencing on the Commencement Date the Company shall initially pay a base salary to the Executive at a rate of $155,000 per annum, with such salary being subject to annual increases by the Board (such base salary as in effect from time to time being referred to as the "Base Salary"). The Base Salary shall be paid in monthly installments, or in such other periodic method as is consistent with Company's standard payroll practice. . . .

3.5 Compensation Cap. Notwithstanding anything to the contrary contained elsewhere in this Agreement, the salary and bonuses paid to the Executive pursuant to Sections 3.1, 3.2, 3.3, and 3.4 above, shall be subject to an aggregate compensation cap as follows:

a. $275,000 for fiscal years ended December 31, 2001 and 2002;
b. $300,000 for fiscal year ended December 31, 2003; and
c. $400,000 for fiscal year ended December 31, 2004.

Executive's Insight: Salary Negotiations

Cale Graham is vice president of strategic planning with a major financial services provider. Here, he discusses his experience negotiating salary for a new position. The win–win principles exemplified in this excerpt are shown in the right-hand margin of the text.

"I moved from a position as director in the product development group to vice president of the retail group. The two groups are essentially separate companies within the parent company. My new boss knew me, and wanted me in the role. The challenging part of the negotiation was that the people in HR didn't seem to want to pay what I thought the job was worth. I had to first determine whether or not my new boss had the same evaluation of the job as I did, and if so, to convince HR to pay me more.

Principles in Action: Identify the core problem.

"For many jobs within the company, HR ultimately controls compensation. They are responsible for making sure like jobs are paid like amounts, and they can say whether or not a certain job can be paid a certain amount, but they work through the hiring managers. So my potential new boss was the one who put the offer in front of me, and I started negotiating with him, but he then had to go back to HR if something didn't work from my perspective. We had talked about the qualifications for the job, I interviewed with folks internally, and they put an offer on the table—but it wasn't what I felt I needed to be paid to do this job.

Principles in Action: Identify your needs.

"Part of my decision was based on my own bottom line, the things I need to pay for every month. But there was also another element. At the time, I had also been interviewing externally. I had several very warm leads, and one that was hot: They were prepared to put an offer on the table, and they had already indicated what they were willing to pay. Early in the negotiations, I had told them, 'Let's not waste everybody's time here. Let me just say up front that if you're not willing to pay at least this amount, we shouldn't be talking.' That's a tough one to do, because you're showing some of your hand, but you pick an amount that's more than you can live with, but that is not exorbitant. I took that approach because I didn't want to spend a lot of time on the interview process and then find that the compensation was not acceptable to me.

Principles in Action: Identify your BATNA.

"At the same time, I was interviewing internally, and this vice president offer came through. All other things being equal, it made sense to take the in-house offer. There's a vesting period for 401(k) and other retirement money, so if you keep an internal job that pays just about as much,

Principles in Action: Look at the compensation package as a whole.

you ultimately come out ahead financially because you have completed the vesting period.

"Because the whole thing came up very quickly, I didn't have a lot of time to prepare for the negotiation. Basically, my new boss said, 'I want to make you an offer, here it is.' I told my boss, 'I'm sorry, but that's just not enough to satisfy the obligations I have to my family. I know the amount I'm asking for is reasonable, because I have another job offer in the works from an outside company, and it's significantly more than this.'

"My boss was very straightforward with me. He said, 'This is not my view of the level of this job, it's HR's view. I agree with you, I think there's a lot of potential in the job.' He even took the next step with me. He said, 'I think you need to take this up with HR yourself. I can't get them to move from their position, but I think you might be able to. Make it clear to them that you've got a firm offer, and that if we can't match the other offer, you'll take it.' He gave me the name of the HR person he was talking with, and then he called her and told her what was happening.

"So she called me. Actually, it was a three-way conversation, with two people from HR on one end of the line, and me on the other. They tried every way under the sun to make me see the value of the package they had put out there. They went into all the additional benefits the company offers, and asked if I had looked at the outside firm's offer as thoroughly, did it really include these kinds of health benefits, these kinds of insurance benefits, these kinds of potential bonus opportunities. Now, of course, I hadn't yet gone into all the details with the other company, but we had talked about base salary and the bonus pool I would be in. So I said to the HR people, 'No, I don't know about the insurance and everything else, but if you're going to be competitive in hiring, those things are somewhat standard. However, they said they are willing to give me this much in terms of salary, and they are putting me in this bonus pool,' which was comparable to what HR was talking about. But they still tried to push the offer, saying, 'We think this is a great opportunity for you to grow and get some exposure, you really would be giving up a lot to go to a different company now, the whole vesting schedule and everything else.' I

Principles in Action: Focus on interests, not positions.

said, 'I hear you. But what I need you to hear is that I'm looking at this alternative because it can help me meet my monthly obligations, and what I'm not hearing from you is an awareness that I need to make a certain amount each month to meet my obligations. If you can't give me that amount, that's fine, no hard feelings. I just need you to understand that there's a base level below which I don't have any flexibility. We can talk about this until we're blue in the face, but that aspect of it will not change.'

Principles in Action: Communicate clearly.

"Finally, they said 'OK, let's think about it, and we'll get back to you.' Then, later that day, they called me back and made me an offer that was less than what the other folks were offering, but significantly more than they had put on the table originally. I had been asking for an increase of about 30 percent from my current position, and they came in at around 25 percent, which was a big step for them. I really don't think they could have done any more than 25 percent without having to clear some internal hurdles.

"There were several challenges to this negotiation. The first one was raising the subject of money to begin with. You know, that's pretty hard for people to do. But once you start doing it, you learn to get a little better at it. The second challenge was trying to find a balance in the negotiation. I didn't want to antagonize them, because they held all the cards, but I wanted to keep things moving along. And there were two of them, doing a kind of a tag team thing; it would have been easy to get frustrated and cave in to them. So I had to have the persistence to keep resisting their offer without making them angry in the process. If I'd made them angry, they could easily have said 'No, we can't pay that much, your boss will just have to find somebody else to hire.'

Principles in Action: Make the discussion a win–win process.

Principles in Action: Be persistent, but flexible.

"Essentially, I think we reached an acceptable solution for several reasons. One was that I was both patient and persistent. Another was that I found arguments that they could relate to. Part of that involved having some familiarity with them, and their approaches to things. People in HR often tend to fall into one of two groups: analysts, or nurturers. The analysts look at the logistics of jobs, and keep track of turnover. The nurturers tend to care about the well-being of individual employees, and are concerned with resolving conflicts. They realize that the way an employee feels about the way he or she is treated can affect the way the job is performed. The woman in charge of the negotiations definitely fell into the latter group; she was in HR because she liked the human aspect of it. So I felt she would respond well if I couched my arguments in terms of human needs. I stressed the fact that my request wasn't about 'wanting' more money, it was about 'needing.' It was about taking care of my family, and meeting a base level of need.

Principles in Action: Adapt your message to fit the other person's style.

"Also, before I went into the negotiation, I was willing to walk away from it if my requests were not met. I had a very good alternative lined up, so if the in-house negotiation didn't work out, I would be better off taking the alternative, rather than backing down on what I had asked for. Knowing this made it easier for me to be firm, to hold to my position. And it affected them, too—they realized that I could just say, 'It's not enough, I'm going to take the other offer.' They realized that they couldn't play hardball and say, 'See you later, when you change your mind.' I wouldn't be around later. I think that really struck a chord with them. Again, I was very straightforward with them. I told them what the other job was, named the firm and the position, told them the amount. I didn't try to match the two jobs up point by point—I didn't have the information to do that—but enough so they knew it wasn't pie in the sky, the sort of situation where you've had an initial interview and a job offer might come out of it, or might not.

Principles in Action: Be ready to walk away if your needs aren't met.

"All in all, I'd say that any negotiation is about perspective. You need to understand the other side's perspective, and to have a pretty firm grasp of your own—the difference between what you want and what you need. Understanding the other person's perspective is key. In my discussion with my boss, I needed to know whether the salary he was offering me was his perspective of what the job was

Principles in Action: Understand the other party's perspective.

worth; getting the answer to that question took any adversarial aspect out of negotiating with him. In fact, he ended up helping me negotiate for what I wanted! In my negotiation with the people from HR, I knew that one of them tended to look at things from a human perspective, so I focused on that aspect in my discussion. The whole thing is about understanding perspectives, and adjusting your arguments to address them.

"And once you understand the other party's perspective, you are more likely to be able to think through the types of arguments they're likely to bring, and to prepare your responses. You can't prepare for everything; some things are going to be a surprise, and you need to be quick on your feet. But if you've already covered four of the five arguments in your mind, then the one that surprises you is only 20 percent of the issue. If you have to think on your feet for everything, you're going to be overwhelmed, but you can improvise for 20 percent. This also helps you be patient and persistent, and keep your cool. Negotiations aren't the place for emotions.

Principles in Action: Anticipate the other party's objections.

Principles in Action: Maintain self-control and composure.

"Negotiation is about getting the job done, so if you don't get in the door this way, let's come around the other side and see if we can get in this window. Let's keep going around until we find an opening."

Chapter Summary: Salary

- **Prepare. Prepare. Prepare.** Collect salary data for an equivalent position in a similar-sized company in the same industry and geographic location.
- **Know what you want. Understand what they want. Know what you need.** The play in the negotiation is between what you need and what you want. If you get less than you need, then the negotiation has not been successful.
- **Avoid putting the first salary figure on the table.** Always wait for the company to make the first offer.

- **Make your salary discussion a win–win process.** Avoid confrontation. It's not wise to negotiate hard on everything; choose what's most important to you.
- **Be creative and agile.** There are many ways to arrive at a mutually beneficial solution, so be prepared to propose and discuss various alternative compensation options.
- **Identify your alternative.** Always have a second choice.
- **Be prepared to walk away.** If your needs aren't being met, be willing to walk away.

CHAPTER FIVE

Stock Options

> *Most elements of a stock options package really aren't negotiable up front. . . . If you change the provisions for one person, you hurt the integrity of the whole plan; you really have to give everyone the same provisions.*
>
> —Joan Williams, CFO

◆ The Challenge and Overview

Stock options can considerably increase an executive's compensation package. However, they can also be a financial pitfall. The possibility of a stock options windfall can persuade an executive to accept a lower salary package. Then, if the anticipated stock surge doesn't take place, the financial downside can be considerable.

Essentially, a stock option gives an employee the right to buy a certain amount of company stock at a given price. If the market price of the stock is higher than the price the employee pays for the stock, then the employee can sell the stock for a profit.

Example: Kazuyo Shimada accepted a position at Startupdotcom, a new Internet-based business, in 1995. Because the company was a start-up, they were trying to keep current costs down. They offered Kazuyo a salary of $75,000, plus 5,000 shares of company stock at a price of $10 per share, to be available after four years. In 1999, when Kazuyo was able to exercise his option, the dotcom boom was at its height. Kazuyo bought 5,000 shares at the price the company had offered him at hiring—$10 per share—for a total cost of $50,000. As soon as the waiting period was over, he sold the stock; the market price was now $135 a share, so the 5,000 shares sold for $675,000, or a profit of $625,000.

Companies use stock options as an incentive to potential employees: Join our company and you may be able to accrue a substantial investment in just a few years. However, the incentive doesn't come without conditions. While stock options are usually part of the hiring agreement, the options don't become available immediately. The options package usually includes a *vesting schedule*, which indicates when the employee can exercise the option. A common schedule is to have 25 percent of the options become available after each of the first four years of employment. This is sometimes referred to as a schedule with *annual cliffs* or *cliff vesting.*

Another condition often imposed is an *options expiration date:* If you don't exercise your options before this date, the options expire. After the expiration date, you can purchase stock only on the open market, at the market price.

A third safeguard is a *holding period* before the employee can sell the stock. This is used both to encourage employees to keep their stock in the company, which can foster a sense of ownership, and to reduce volatility in the company's stock, which can occur if employees exercise their options one day, buying a large block of stock, then immediately turn around and sell the stock.

The final safeguard usually included in the options package makes the options contingent on continued employment. If the executive leaves before the end of the vesting period, all unvested options automatically expire.

All of these conditions are imposed to protect the company's investment in the employee. However, there is another condition that greatly affects the value of an options package: the state of the market. As discussed above, a stock options package usually includes several variables. The *grant price,* or *strike price,* is the price at which the company agrees to let the employee buy stock; this is often based on the actual market price at the time the employee is hired. The *vesting period* is the length of time the employee must wait before being able to exercise the option and purchase the stock. And the *expiration date* is the date when the options expire. When the executive agrees to the options package, it is in the hope that the value of the company's stock will rise between the time the grant price is set and the time the options are exercised. However, the options can usually be exercised only within a specific period of time. If the market price of the stock during that time is below the grant price (sometimes referred to as being "under water"), then the options are worthless.

> ***Example:*** When Alicia Hall joined Best Options in 1997, the market price of the company's stock was $78 a share. She negotiated an options package for a total of 4,000 shares, to vest over four years. The options would remain available for one year after the end of the vesting period; then they would expire. Unfortunately for Alicia, when the vesting period ended, in 2001, the stock market as a whole was down; the market price for Best Options was hovering at around $35. Throughout the twelve months that her options remained exercisable, Alicia watched prices closely, but Best Options never rose above $42. Since Alicia's strike price was $78, there was no point in exercising the option before it expired. The stock options element of Alicia's employment package ended up being valueless.

The first challenge in negotiating a stock options package is taking into account the many different variables and maintaining a realistic viewpoint. Remember, you cannot pay your living expenses with stock options, so it's also important that you negotiate hard first on the salary and benefits part of your package before you agree to a stock options package.

The second big challenge when negotiating a stock options package involves minimizing your tax obligations on the gain—the difference between the strike price and the value of the stock. To further complicate this issue, the two common types of stock plans are subject to distinctly different tax regulations. The section that follows gives a general overview of the two types of stock option plans and the tax liabilities for each; however, because of the complexity of this topic, you should consult a tax expert about your specific situation before making any decisions.

The final challenge of this negotiation is that few of the provisions in a stock options plan can be changed. Elements such as the vesting schedule are the same for all employees in the plan. The biggest negotiable element is the number of options you receive. In order to receive as many options as possible, you need to understand how stock options work. A useful resource for detailed information about stock options is the book *Better Than Money: Build Your Fortune Using Stock Options and Equity Incentives—in Up* and *Down Markets,* by David Gumpert (2000; Lauson Publishing Co., P.O. Box 36, Needham, MA).

The Two Types of Stock Options

There are two types of stock options: *incentive stock options* (ISOs) and *nonqualified stock options* (NSOs). These two types of options differ considerably in terms of who is eligible to receive them and how they are taxed. Incentive stock options (ISOs) are only granted to employees, whereas nonqualified stock options (NSOs) can be handed out to anyone, such as consultants, contractors, or outside directors.

Incentive Stock Options (ISOs)

These plans are designed, as the name suggests, to provide an incentive for employees. They cannot be given to consultants or other contractors. These plans are also sometimes referred to as "qualified" stock options, because they qualify for special tax treatment. No income tax is due when you receive the options, or even when you exercise them; the tax is deferred until you sell the stock. And then, if you observe the minimum waiting periods—one year between receiving the options and exercising them, and one year between exercise and sale of the stock—your gain is taxed as long-term capital gain, rather than as ordinary income. This usually results in a smaller tax liability than if the gain were treated as either income or short-term capital gain.

However, if you don't meet the holding period requirements, the sale of the stock is considered a "disqualifying disposition," and you are taxed as if you had held nonqualified options: the spread at exercise (between strike price and exercise price) is taxed as ordinary income.

In terms of tax liabilities for the employee (discussed in more detail starting on page 67), ISOs are by far the more favorable of the two types of plans. However, there are four things to keep in mind about ISOs:

- A maximum of $100,000 in ISOs can become exercisable in any year.
- If the holding period requirements aren't met, the gain is taxed as if the options were NSOs.
- The spread at exercise is considered a preference item for calculating Alternative Minimum Tax (AMT).
- ISOs must usually be exercised within ninety days of termination of employment, whether voluntary or involuntary, which can affect your tax liabilities.

Nonqualified Stock Options (NSOs)

With nonqualified stock options, when you exercise the option, the difference between the grant price and the exercise price is taxed as income—even if you haven't yet sold the stock and realized the income. Then, when you do sell the stock, any appreciation over the exercise price is taxed at capital gain rates. Again, certain minimum holding periods affect your tax liability. If you sell the stock within a year of exercising the option, the gain will be viewed as short-term capital gain; if you hold it for more than a year after exercise, the gain will be treated as long-term, and will be taxed at a lower rate.

Even if you decide not to sell the stock, you'll have to pay taxes. When you decide to exercise the option, you have to pay for the cost of the stock as well as applicable withholding taxes, which can include federal, state, and FICA.

The advantage to employers of NSO plans is that the company is able to deduct the spread between the grant price and the exercise price as a compensation expense. Thus, employers tend to offer NSO plans to the rank and file, while reserving ISO plans for a small cadre of top-level employees. Also, unlike ISOs, which can only be granted to employees, nonqualified options can be offered to consultants, contractors, or other nonemployees.

◆ Preparation

As with all other areas of the job negotiation process, with stock options, preparation is essential. Before you negotiate an options package, you need to have a lot of information—about the company, the industry, and yourself. It's important not only to prepare the relevant questions in advance but also to understand the answers you're given in order to respond appropriately. Don't let yourself be swayed by rosy visions of the possible future value of the shares; your negotiation should be based on the here-and-now—the value of the shares today.

With stock options, there are no guarantees, but doing your homework will help you evaluate the costs and benefits. Again, before making any decisions about a specific stock options package, it is important to consult a tax professional, as the tax ramifications can be considerable.

Know the Company

When you agree to a stock options package, in essence, you are betting that the value of the company's stock will go up before you exercise your options. Before you make that bet, you need to evaluate the odds that you will win. Before buying stock in a company, you would do a careful analysis of the company's track record and predictions for its future. When you agree to a stock options package, you are investing yourself in the "stock purchase"; make sure you have the information you need to get a good return on your investment. This includes being fully informed about the company's management team, current revenues, annual growth rate, and profitability.

A young start-up company can offer exciting opportunities, but it also offers increased risk. Statistically, the odds against your bet paying off are greater with a start-up than with an established company. If the company is new, find out as much as you can about the background and track record of the principals. Has the CEO led a string of failed companies, or several successful ventures? Does the company have adequate capitalization? What is the source of its funding?

In the case of an established company, especially one that is publicly traded, the evaluation is often easier as the company has an available track record. Start by looking at the company's most recent annual report. Then look for analysts' reports on the company. If the company's earnings have been below expectations for several quarters, or if its cash position has been declining, then any options you receive may have little value for some time to come. An interesting indicator of a company's health is the number of employees a company has recently hired. If you scan the newspapers and visit the company's Web site, you can see the number and types of positions they are looking to fill. Check within your network for anyone who has worked for the company; current and former employees can often give you useful information about the company's internal health.

If a company is privately held, solid financial information may be harder to come by. Earnings reports are less likely to be available, and the company may not be willing to share such information with you. During the interview, try to establish whether the company has been expanding, or has had to institute layoffs. Ask about the company's capitalization. A company may ask you to sign a nondisclosure agreement before discussing its capitalization with you; this is perfectly reasonable. (For more information on nondisclosure agreements, see Chapter Nine.) However, if a company refuses to discuss its capitalization, be wary of accepting an offer from them. One way to learn more about a company's current focus is to inquire about the types of positions the company is currently hiring for. If you find that they are only hiring salespeople, and are not filling any positions in administration or support roles, that may provide reason for further probing; in times of growth, you need those other functions to help support the addition of new clients. A focus on sales staff may indicate a need for increased revenue, without an adequate plan for achieving it.

You should also ask about the company's future fund-raising plans, and whether additional shares have been authorized. If you receive an option on 100 shares and the company has 1,000 shares outstanding, your 10 percent share could be worth a lot if the company goes public or is acquired. However, if the company needs to raise cash before going public, it may issue more stock, diluting the value of your stake. Another cause of dilution may be preferred shareholders with the option to convert to common stock. Since dilution can affect the value of your options, you should know as much about it as possible before entering into an agreement.

Know the Industry

The strength of an industry as a whole has a significant effect on the growth of individual companies within that sector. Read research reports on the industry and see what kind of growth rate analysts are predicting. While individual companies can certainly outperform the industry as a whole, when predicting the potential growth of a company's stock price, industry-wide growth is a good predictor of individual company growth. It is useful to go to one of the news services that offer sector-specific information, such as www.individual.com, and try to understand the sector. Look at research articles through on-line sites such as Gartner (www.gartner.com) and Edgar Online (www.edgar-online.com), which have research and articles to help you understand a specific sector. If you've identified a publicly traded company for potential employment, investment companies such as Schwab and Fidelity have sector watch reports by category, which list all key companies; determine which ones are growing and which aren't, then analyze the trends for that sector.

The market is one of the best indicators of the efficiency of revenue or capital in a particular area. Overall market trends tell us a lot about an industry, because the capital markets are fickle and can change quickly on a rumor. A thirty- to sixty-day decline in a particular market would raise some questions; you should inquire about such occurrences in your employment discussions.

Know Yourself

Before negotiating for stock options, it's important to understand your own comfort level with risk. An aggressive stock options package with a start-up company could be worth a great deal—or could be worth nothing at all. How well prepared are you, both financially and in terms of your temperament, for taking on risk? If you are not comfortable with risk, or have extensive financial commitments, it may be preferable to negotiate a package that includes a higher salary and fewer options. Then you can invest the additional salary in a stock portfolio of your own choosing without having to wait for your options to be vested.

Once you know your level of risk tolerance, it's important to have a clear idea of your own value. Based on your skills and experience, what kind of salary could you reasonably expect? You can then use your "market value" to negotiate a complete compensation package. For example, if you know you're worth $100,000 a year and you're offered a salary of $75,000, you should negotiate an options package, based on the stock's current value, worth $25,000 a year for the vesting period. If your vesting period is four years, that would require an options package with a current value of $100,000.

> ***Example:*** Finbarr Lawlor, a Web developer, knew that the going salary for people with his skills and experience was $95,000. WebWorks offered him a salary of $70,000, and options at a strike price of $35, with a three-year vesting period. The difference between the salary Finbarr knew he should get and the offer WebWorks made him was $25,000 a year. Over the three-year vesting period, that would come to $75,000. Finbarr negotiated for the option to buy 2,200 shares at the $35 strike price. At the time of hiring, these options had a value of $77,000—just $2,000 more than the $75,000 salary differential.

Know the Tax Consequences

The tax consequences of a stock options package will depend on many things: your tax bracket, the type of options you have, and the company's situation. As the examples below show, changing the variables can dramatically change the tax liability.

ISO, Observing the Holding Period

> ***Example:*** Sunder Hammond joined an early-stage, privately owned software company on June 23, 1999, and received options for 20,000 shares of stock at 20 cents a share. Under the company's four-year vesting schedule, 5,000 of his options vested after the first year. He exercised his vested options and purchased 5,000 shares on June 25, 2000, for $1,000. Within a week of his purchase, the company went public at $25 a share. On June 26,

> 2001, with the stock still at $25 a share, he sold his 5,000 shares, and received $125,000, for a gain of $124,000.

In the ideal situation, Sunder would have had a simple long-term gain in this transaction of $124,000, incurring a maximum federal tax of 20 percent on the $124,000 (or $24,800). But there is a possibility that he could have to pay income tax on the $124,000 difference in price between the original 20-cents-a-share price of the options in mid-1999 and the $25 per share value of the options when he exercised them in June 2000. This is due to the Alternative Minimum Tax (AMT). The AMT basically recalculates an individual's tax liability by eliminating deductions and including certain events as income—such as the exercise of stock options—and then applying a flat percentage tax rate. If the AMT liability exceeds the tax liability under your tax return calculation, then you would be liable for the difference. The implications of the Alternative Minimum Tax differ from individual to individual; for specifics, you should consult a tax expert.

ISO, Not Observing the Holding Period

In the example above, Sunder followed the provisions of the holding period. He waited one year between being granted the options and exercising them, and waited another year between exercising the options and selling the stocks. However, if he needed to realize the income before the end of the twelve-month holding period, or felt that the value of the company's stock was likely to fall dramatically, he might decide that receiving a higher stock price was worth accepting the greater tax liabilities of ignoring the holding period. He might choose to exercise the options as soon as they vested, then sell the stock immediately.

> ***Example:*** Sunder joined the company on June 23, 1999, and received options for 20,000 shares of stock at 20 cents a share. Under the company's four-year vesting schedule, 5,000 of his options vested after the first year. He purchased 5,000 shares on June 25, 2000, for $1,000. On October 17, 2000, the company went public at $25 a share. Sunder immediately sold his 5,000 shares at that price, and received $125,000, a gain of $124,000.

Because Sunder held the stock for less than a year, his gain of $124,000 is treated as ordinary income, not long-term gain. This means he pays federal taxes at his ordinary highest rate—usually 28 percent to 33 percent. If his federal obligation is 33 percent, his tax will be about $40,920, or $16,120 more than if he had observed the holding period.

Nonqualified Stock Options

With nonqualified stock options, the biggest tax challenge is the fact that you must pay taxes as soon as you exercise the option. Because of this, one approach is to wait as long as possible before exercising your options and creating a tax liability. In most companies, the options remain open for up to ten years from the date of issue (unless you leave the company). This means that you can follow the company's performance in the long term before deciding on a good time to purchase the stock.

An exception to this approach would be a situation where a company's stock hasn't appreciated much above the grant price, but a big advance is likely in the near future. In such a case, it would be worth paying immediate taxes on the spread in order to set yourself up in a long-term capital gain situation.

Example: Eve Baker joined a small private PR firm, and was given 2,000 options at 50 cents a share. Now, two years later, 1,000 of her options have vested. The company is still private, and the valuation is 75 cents a share. However, Eve feels confident that, within a year or two, the company will have an initial public offering, which could make the stock worth $15 or $20 a share. She decides that it's worth paying taxes on the gain, which is only $250 (1,000 shares with a gain of 25 cents a share). If she waited until the company went public and the stock prices rose to $15, she would have to pay on the spread between 50 cents and $15—a total of $14,500 (1,000 shares with a gain of $14.50 a share). If she buys the stocks now, any later appreciation will be taxed as capital gain, not income.

Understand Option Forfeiture

Understanding the trigger events that would lead to forfeiture of stock options is important, because this dictates the time frame in which you actually earn the right to purchase your options and the specific dates where your options cannot be forfeited. For example, assume that, when you joined the company, you were granted 40,000 options with annual vesting over a four-year period, which means that you would earn the right to purchase 10,000 options each year. After two years, you would have earned the right to purchase a total of 20,000 options. If you leave the company after twenty-eight months, you will forfeit or lose your right to purchase the additional 20,000 options because you did not stay with the company for the entire four-year period. Additionally, the 20,000 options that have vested could be affected by provisions like those described below.

Change of Ownership

If the company is acquired, your unvested options may be lost. It is important to include a clause stating that, in the event that the company is acquired, all unvested options immediately vest and become eligible for exercise.

Termination

Some agreements include a provision stating that you lose all your unexercised vested options if you leave the company before the entire vesting period ends. If your agreement includes this type of provision, you should try to negotiate for a change so that, if you leave the company due to an involuntary termination, all options vest and become eligible for exercise.

Purchase Window upon Leaving the Company or Termination

All incentive stock options agreements include an expiration clause that specifies when your options expire, typically five to seven years from the time the options are granted. However, if you leave the company voluntarily or if you are terminated, you typically have a ninety-day window to decide if you want to exercise your right to purchase your options. Even if all your options have vested, you could lose them if you don't exercise them within this window.

Options Exercise Period

All options have a time limit on how long they last; the exercise period runs from the time the options are granted until a specified expiration date. This can range from five to ten years. If your options are "under water"—the market price of the stock is below the exercise price—you would want to wait until a later date to exercise your options. However, if you wait, you should be aware of the limitations of your exercise period.

Establish Your Salary First

Before you start discussing an options package, it's important to have a final salary figure. Why? Because while salary and options are both compensation, they cannot be evaluated in the same way. Your salary has a real, fixed value; if you negotiate a salary of $104,000 a year, then you know that you will have a gross pay of $2,000 a week. Options, on the other hand, have an intangible value. Just because a stock is selling at $82 a share when you are hired doesn't guarantee that it will be selling for more—or even as much—when you are able to exercise your options. If you discuss both salary and options together, there is a risk that you will lose sight of the difference between real and potential compensation, and will accept a lower salary as part of a total compensation package. Until your options have vested, you can't use them to meet your financial obligations. Make sure you know what the salary will be first.

Another advantage of finalizing the salary first is that you may be able to use your salary to negotiate for more options.

> ***Example:*** Margaret Lyscars has been offered a position at a young company, with a salary of $60,000 and options worth $20,000, on a four-year vesting schedule. With $5,000 worth of options vesting each year, this would bring her first-year compensation up to $65,000. However, her research indicated that an appropriate salary for this position should be closer to $80,000. She used her salary, and the objective criteria she had provided as part of the salary negotiation, to negotiate for options worth $60,000.

◆ The Negotiation

Before you can evaluate a stock options package, you need to know all the variables: number of outstanding shares, strike price, current market value, vesting period, minimum holding period, and options expiration date. Agreeing to an options package without knowing all this information is like signing a mortgage loan agreement without knowing the principal and interest on the loan. The questions below will help you determine the essentials in a discussion of stock options.

Analysis

Analyze the situation, your interests, and those of the other party, and begin gathering information. Consider your own interests, and those of the other party, by doing a self-analysis and an opportunity analysis. You will need to develop answers to questions like these:

Key Questions

Self-Analysis

- How willing am I to accept the risk (and potential upside) of stock options?
- If this company were not my employer, would I invest in it?
- What is a fair market value for my services?
- Does the combined compensation package—salary plus stock options—give me the total compensation I should be receiving?
- How will the stock options offered affect my taxes?

Opportunity Analysis

- What is the company's financial track record?
- What do analysts say about the industry in general, and this company in particular?
- How is stock offered (options, stock purchase plan, employee stock ownership program)?

Planning

Use planning to establish your strategy, understand the other party's interests, and determine what options or alternatives would be acceptable outcomes. Ask yourself questions like these as part of your planning process:

Key Questions

- Does the person I'm negotiating with understand enough about stock options to have an in-depth discussion?
- Do I understand enough about options to have an in-depth discussion?
- Is the company proud of its employee ownership?
- How widespread is employee ownership at the company? Is it only for the management team, or is everyone eligible for stock ownership?
- Is stock used as a recruiting tool instead of a higher cash-based salary?
- How long do I intend to work for the company? Does my timeline match the vesting schedule for the stock options, or could I end up forfeiting some of my options?

Discussion

During the negotiation, you can gather new information in two ways: through questions you ask the interviewer, and through unsolicited information the interviewer shares as part of the discussion. These are some of the questions you should ask and information you should listen for:

Questions to Ask

- How many people has the company hired during the past year?
- How do you expect to pay for these employees? (Beware of answers indicating that the company expects an increased staff to generate the revenue needed to finance growth.)

- What is the specific number of stock options offered?
- Will the options be ISOs (incentive stock options) or NSOs (nonqualified stock options)?
- What is the upside potential?
- What is the estimated time frame?
- What is the plan for increasing the value of the stock?
- What time frame do the primary owners have for initiating a liquidity event (merger, sale, or IPO that will convert stock into more liquid assets)?
- How many outstanding shares are there in the company?
- What are the company's future fund-raising plans?
- What are the risks of stock dilution?
- What is the strike price?
- What is the basis for the strike price?
- What is the current market price?
- How long is the vesting period?
- What are the incremental vesting periods—annual, quarterly, monthly, etc.?
- What is the expiration date for the options?
- If the company is acquired, do my options automatically vest?
- Can I earn additional options for each year I am with the company?
- Can I see a copy of the Stock Option Plan?

Information to Listen For

- Does the company's management team have a sound strategy for building the company's value?
- If it's a privately held company, is there a clear plan for converting stock into a more liquid asset (through acquisition or IPO)?

◆ Outcome: Next Steps

Once you have negotiated your equity or stock options positions, it's time to capture the terms in your employment contract. The contract should explicitly state the number of shares you will receive in the Incentive Stock Option Grant Agreement, as shown below.

This agreement will also contain the vesting schedule for your stock options. This is a critical component because it dictates when you will be able to purchase the shares outright. Vesting schedules can vary from one year to five years; also, vesting periods can be monthly, quarterly, or annually. Illustrated below is a sample four-year vesting schedule with annual cliffs—that is, 25 percent of the shares are vested each year for four years. The executive in this agreement will earn the right to purchase 18,170 shares annually, at a predefined price per share.

The clause that follows the vesting schedule states that the shares will fully vest if there is a change in control. This is an important clause to include. Without such a clause, you could be only 25 or 50 percent vested at the time of acquisition, and thus might lose the big upside potential.

Example as Excerpted from an Executive's Employment Agreement

3.6 Stock. Concurrently with the signing of this Agreement, the Company shall grant to the Executive 18,170 shares of the Company's common stock subject to a Stock Restriction Agreement in substantially the form attached hereto as Exhibit A.

3.7 Stock Option. The Executive shall be entitled to participate in the Company's stock option plan, established or to be established by the Board or other such plan as created from time to time by the Board. Initially, the Executive shall be granted an option to purchase 72,680 shares of the Company's Common Stock. The terms and conditions of grant and exercise governing such option shall be as set forth in the form of Incentive Stock Option Grant Agreement attached hereto as Exhibit B.

Sample Stock Vesting Schedule

Period from employment date	*Vested Percentage*	*Unvested Percentage*
Less than one year	0%	100%
One year but less than two years	25%	75%
Two years but less than three years	50%	50%
Three years but less than four years	75%	25%
Four years or longer	100%	0%

The options shall fully vest at any such time that the Company is purchased by another company or institutes a public offering of shares. Prior to any stock purchase, the Member will be required to execute a copy of the Company's Shareholders Agreement.

Executive's Insight: Stock Options

Joan Williams started her career in corporate banking. She later became treasurer, then CFO, of U.S. News and World Report. *Since then, she has been CFO and CEO of several start-up companies. Here, she discusses her experience negotiating stock options. The win–win principles exemplified in this excerpt are shown in the right-hand margin of the text.*

"As a CFO, I've negotiated stock options from both sides—as employee and as employer. The first time I was offered stock options, I knew nothing, and didn't negotiate anything. I essentially accepted what they offered me. (Although I did negotiate for more salary.) I knew what stock options were, but my perception was that they would have value only if we were able to take the company public.

"By the time I came to negotiate the options at subsequent positions, I had learned more about what the market was. I knew, for instance, that a CFO, depending on the stage of the company, could get anywhere from 1 to 3 percent of the company in options, in fully diluted shares. The question of stock options is usually raised as part of the overall compensation question—salary, bonuses, options, and so forth. The employer usually wants to know what the compensation is in total. And I've always given an honest answer. When I'm negotiating, I don't see it as being based so much on what I was making before as what my contribution will be and how I fit into the organization. In fact, at one company, I was hired at a certain level at a time when the company's finances were tight. The CEO and founder said, 'Here's what all of us at this level are getting in options, and here's what we are getting in salary,' and there was essentially a cap on both options and salary; it was a function of where the company was and what we were doing. There wasn't a lot of room for negotiation. But I was excited about the opportunity; I liked the idea, and I liked the founder, so I said OK. Then, a few months later, I went back to him and said, 'OK, since I came on board we've raised money, and I've proved myself. We've increased our option pool, and now I want X number of options.' To decide on a number, I looked at the contribution I was making as compared to the contribution others in the organization were making. I knew what my strike price was, and I knew what I thought we might go public at. Also, I talked with my accounting firm to get their input. I put all that together to come up with a figure. And because I had proved myself, he agreed.

Principles in Action:
Look at the options package as part of the overall compensation plan.

"Most elements of a stock options package really aren't negotiable up front. One thing that I have negotiated in my last two positions is a double trigger. The first trigger is a change of control, the second is that I get fired or demoted. If those two events occur, then my options vest. Given my position, that provision is important to me. If the company changes ownership, the first person who gets fired is the CFO, just because the new company wants to put their own financial person in to find out what's going on. And so, as a CFO, I will not take a job without a double trigger.

"But apart from that, you can't negotiate most of the provisions, like the vesting period, and so forth. If you change the provisions for one person, you hurt the integrity of the whole plan. You really have to give everyone the same provisions.

"When I'm getting ready to negotiate the stock options, the first thing I would do is sign an NDA, a nondisclosure agreement, stating that I wouldn't disclose any information the company shared with me as part of this process. Then I would ask to read the company's stock options plan, so that I understand what the plan says before I start negotiating. And then I would ask questions about their fund-raising, such as, 'What was your last round? If you had a last round, how much did you raise in it? Was it a series A, B, C? What is the current strike price on your options?'

Principles in Action: Know the company.

"One goal of asking questions like these is to get a sense of where the company is in the view of the investors. Was the valuation of the last round $3 million, or $15 million? A company with a valuation of $15 million is in a very different place from a company with a valuation of $3 million.

"Then, in looking at the plan, I like to see what the vesting period is. Is it a cliff plan, with a one-year cliff and then monthly vesting, or are there annual cliffs? I far prefer monthly vesting after the first year, rather than annual vesting periods. I look to see whether or not they have a change-of-control provision in there, and what it says. Some change-of-control provisions say that the options vest only if the acquiring company doesn't assume the plan or exchanges it for stock of their own or something, which is not a very strong provision.

"In general, when you're preparing to negotiate on stock options, you have to look at compensation as a total package. The first thing is to decide what's important to you. In some cases, I've been more interested in salary, and in others I've been more interested in options. A lot of that has to do with where I am in my life at the time.

"Even if I don't expect to get the answers, there are certain questions that I'll ask. How many shares are outstanding on a fully diluted basis? What is the vesting schedule: Is it one-year cliff and annual thereafter, or one-year cliff and monthly? Are the options ISOs, or non-qualified options? Unless there was something else very compelling about the company, I would not go for a plan with an annual cliff vesting schedule. The ISO/nonqualified question doesn't affect me as much, because in most cases I'm going to exercise and sell at

Principles in Action: Identify your interests.

the same time, but the vesting schedule would give me pause. It would also make me wonder about the way the management structures other things, because that schedule is not employee-friendly, and is just not very well structured.

"In terms of stock options, the days of getting rich quick are gone. Companies may still try to sell you on that vision, but realistically, very few of those numbers will actually pan out. Depending on your personal situation, I would take options with a grain of salt. They're certainly important, but you need to find out as much as you can about the company's prospects. Then, if you really believe in the company, go for more options. Otherwise, it may be wiser to go for a stronger salary package instead. I'm seeing an increasing number of people who have walked away with worthless options."

Chapter Summary: Stock Options

- **Price per share and total outstanding shares.** Gather this information to determine how much the company is worth and how realistically it is valued.
- **Strike price.** This dictates the price at which you can exercise your options and is important in calculating your prospective gain when evaluating the overall value of your stock options package.
- **Research your investment thoroughly.** Stock options are a financial investment, so do the proper research.
- **Know the company.** Inquire into and analyze the company's track record, management team, current revenues, annual growth rate, and profitability.
- **Know the industry.** Understand the sector trends and perform comparative analysis on similar companies.
- **Know yourself.** Determine your own comfort level with risk: an aggressive stock options package with a start-up company could be worth a great deal—or could be worth nothing at all.

- **Know the tax consequences.** The tax consequences associated with equity compensation are extremely complex; consult a tax expert before exercising a large number of options.
- **Read and understand your stock options agreement.** It's recommended that you review your agreement with an attorney. Carefully review the vesting schedule, strike price, exercise provisions if the company is sold, and termination provisions.

CHAPTER SIX

Signing and Performance Bonuses

I saw the signing bonus almost as a sign of good faith, a sign that they really wanted me.
—Terry Holmes
VP, Sales and Marketing

◆ The Challenge and Overview

A *signing bonus* is a single payout given to the employee when he or she accepts a job. Unlike most other bonuses, a signing bonus is not related to performance. It is simply added compensation to entice an individual to work for the employer. It is also a way to compensate a new employee for expenses that will be incurred as a result of accepting a new job. Signing bonuses average 5 to 10 percent of base salary, depending on the position and industry, but it's not uncommon for top talent to command signing bonuses worth up to 25 percent of their base salaries. Signing bonuses are treated as compensation for income tax purposes and are subject to the same tax withholdings as normal wages. Employers frequently require employees to pay back the bonus if the employee voluntarily terminates his or her employment before a certain time.

A *performance bonus* is a payment made to an employee during a certain period based on achieving specified goals. Performance bonuses can be tied to the performance of the employer or to the performance of the employee. Performance bonus plans are usually in writing and identify specific employment/performance milestones that must be achieved for the bonus to be earned. Performance bonuses are treated as compensation for income tax purposes and are subject to the same tax withholdings as normal wages.

Depending on the situation, performance bonuses can be incorporated into projections of total compensation. It may not be wise to include bonus payouts when creating a budget or financial plan, unless the bonuses are relatively stable from year to year. If you do factor the bonus into personal financial projections, it is wise to use the lower end of the bonus range. In contrast, it is appropriate to include anticipated bonus payments when presenting compensation expectations to a potential employer. Of course, the variability in the bonus amount and the degree to which you have control over the bonus payout (if it's based on individual performance as opposed to company performance) also affect whether it is realistic to include performance bonuses in compensation projections.

◆ Preparation

A signing bonus and performance bonus are typically negotiated as part of your salary negotiations. A smaller company may not be able to meet your salary requirements, but a signing bonus can be used to get an up-front lump-sum payment that demonstrates the company's commitment to you. The signing bonus is also a way for the company to sweeten the deal and show they really want you. Performance bonuses, however, are often easier to negotiate; they are rewards for reaching definite, predefined milestones that increase the overall value of the company. In addition, aggressive performance bonuses are a way to offset a lower salary, as the company is rewarding you for exceptional achievements.

Another advantage of agreeing to performance bonuses as part of the overall compensation package is that it shows the company that you believe in your abilities and you are willing to share the risk the company is taking in hiring you. A prospective employee who insists on complete security by having all compensation based on salary will give the company pause. The employee who is willing to agree to a shared risk scenario will be viewed more favorably.

To prepare for these discussions, you must first determine your overall compensation goals, not necessarily your salary goals. After you've determined your desired compensation level, work backwards to calculate what you will need to reach those goals, based on the salary that is being offered. The additional compensation you will need to reach your goals should be factored into the bonuses.

If you are in sales or are responsible for driving revenues, your bonus plan can be directly tied to gross margin sales (total revenues minus cost of sales). If you are a CFO, your bonus can be tied to net income or profitability levels, especially if you are in a turnaround situation. If you are a CIO, then it can be associated with product development milestones, such as timeliness of bringing product to market. Although you may not be able to suggest a plan before your meeting, because this often requires a collaborative discussion, deciding in advance what you'll need for additional income will make you better prepared to engage in these discussions when they arise.

When deciding whether to negotiate for a signing bonus or a higher base salary, consider the following issues:

- ***Degree to which you need the money up front.*** If you need money to buy a car to get to work or will lose income because of the transition, it may be wise to push for a signing bonus to make up for the initial investment.
- ***Time of year.*** If you're joining a new employer at the end of the year, you may not want a signing bonus that will add significant income to the current tax year. A higher base salary, or a bonus awarded after a certain period of service—e.g., sixty or ninety days—will push the income into the next tax year.
- ***Limitations on base salary.*** While the signing bonus should be viewed as an add-on to base salary, in some cases salary grades may limit the base salary that is offered. A signing bonus could be used to get around salary grades that do not reflect labor market realities.
- ***Your monthly expenses.*** Depending on your monthly expenses, it may be more beneficial to have a higher

base salary spread across each pay period than a lump-sum payment at the beginning of the employment relationship.

- ***Company's cash constraints.*** A start-up company with limited cash flow may find it harder to provide a substantial cash-based signing bonus. Consider alternative forms of compensation, such as a combination of cash bonus and stock options, to achieve a suitable offer.

◆ The Negotiation

As discussed earlier, signing and performance bonuses are most typically negotiated as part of the salary negotiation. Before that meeting, you should determine your overall compensation requirements and establish objective criteria in terms of bonuses for similar positions in your industry.

Decide whether you are looking for a signing bonus, a performance bonus, or both. If seeking both, be prepared to build independent cases for each, because they are quite different. Your signing bonus discussion should be more oriented toward what it would take for you to join the company or the cost or incentives to get you to make a career change. These types of bonuses largely depend upon your leverage—or lack thereof. Your annual or performance bonus discussion should focus around jointly establishing objective measurement criteria that provide for bonuses at specific periods. The goals must be clearly measurable, not based on subjective judgment calls. For example, a gross sales quota is easy to measure, but "getting a product out on time" could be open to interpretation.

We've identified some key areas of the analysis, planning, and discussion phases that you might want to explore before entering this negotiation.

Analysis

Consider your own interests, and those of the other party, by doing a self-analysis and an opportunity analysis. You will need to develop answers to questions like these:

Key Questions

Self-Analysis

- Would I prefer an up-front signing bonus or a higher annual salary?
- To what extent am I comfortable with at-risk compensation?

Opportunity Analysis

- Are the employer's pay levels below the market rate?
- Which offers me the greatest long-term potential, a signing bonus or a performance bonus structure?

Planning

Use planning to establish your strategy, understand the other party's interests, and determine what options or alternatives would be acceptable outcomes. Ask yourself questions like these as part of your planning process:

Key Questions

- What bonus levels are being paid for similar positions within the industry?
- What is the employer's cash situation?
- Is a bonus the only option that will make the offer better than my alternative opportunities?
- Are the goals for the performance bonus objective and easily measurable, or subjective and vaguely defined?

Discussion

During the negotiation, you can obtain new information in two ways: through questions you ask the interviewer, and through unsolicited information the interviewer shares as part of the discussion. These are some of the questions you should ask and some of the information you should listen for:

Questions to Ask

- Does the company offer a signing bonus?
- Does the company offer a performance bonus?

- How frequently is the bonus paid?
- Under what circumstances might a signing bonus have to be paid back to the company?
- What are the criteria for performance bonuses? Are they in writing?
- Is the performance bonus based on individual performance, team/division performance, and/or company performance? To what extent does the individual have control over the level of bonus earned?
- Is the performance bonus based on project-related milestones or financial performance measures such as sales or stock value?
- Who determines whether the goals for performance bonuses have been met?

Information to Listen For

- Are the bonus criteria objective and clearly measurable, or subjective, based on an individual's judgment calls?
- Are the objectives for the position realistic and achievable?

◆ Outcome: Next Steps

Once you have negotiated a bonus structure, you need to capture the terms of those discussions. A signing bonus is straightforward; however, performance bonuses can be quite complex, and each term must be looked at closely by an attorney. It's important to understand the difference between receiving commissions or overrides on net or gross revenues, when the bonuses will be paid, and how frequently. These issues should be discussed while you are negotiating your bonus plan; if they arise while in the contracting phase, remember that you are still in the negotiation process, and continue to lobby for the most favorable terms.

The sample bonus plan that follows includes a variety of performance-based bonuses in a format that is both explicit and fair from the perspectives of both the executive and company.

In this plan, the executive negotiated a $15,000 nonrefundable advance on commissions to offset a slightly lower salary. Since the base salary is $155,000, the $15,000 nonrefundable advance will give the executive $170,000 guaranteed compensation. The company gets the benefit of paying it out over time, while the executive knows that he or she has guaranteed additional compensation.

Although in this case the executive has negotiated a nonrefundable advance, in most situations where an executive receives a signing bonus, the company requires that the executive remain with the company for a certain period of time. The time frame might range from six months to twenty-four months, depending on the overall scope of the position and agreement. Such a clause is a perfectly reasonable request since the company is making a significant outlay of cash. The company wants to ensure that the executive will not leave after three months.

In section 3.2.a the executive has negotiated a 1 percent gross commission override. This means that he or she receives commissions on all sales, except for backing out all returns, discounts, and any third-party license and application fees, which is fair. In this case, all the non-commissionable elements are clearly stated, avoiding any ambiguity. Additionally, sections 3.2.b–3.2.d outline each subsequent year's commission plan.

The quarterly performance bonus terms are clearly stated in section 3.3.a–3.3.d, which presents a defined milestone that relates to a net sales number; if the company reaches that number, the executive will receive a predefined bonus amount. In addition, the bonus payment terms are clearly stated as "30 days after the end of such fiscal quarter."

The last section, 3.4, defines the terms of the executive's annual bonus, which states that the executive "shall be eligible to receive an annual bonus for each calendar year for which the Company has net income, in an amount equal to 15 percent of the net income before taxes." This is designed to cause the executive to focus on profitability as well as increased gross sales. Essentially, the company has implemented a structure that provides twofold incentives: drive overall sales while watching costs and increasing profitability.

Example as Excerpted from an Executive's Employment Agreement

Signing Bonus. Following acceptance of employment with the Company, the Executive shall receive a Signing Bonus in the amount of $____________. This Signing Bonus shall be paid to the Executive at the time of the first payday following the first day of the Executive's employment with the Company. In the event that the Executive voluntarily resigns from employment with the Company prior to the first anniversary date of the Executive's employment with the Company, the Executive shall be required to return the entire Signing Bonus to the Company.

3.2 Annual Company Performance Bonus. Between the Commencement Date and December 31, 2001, the Company shall pay to the Executive an aggregate of $15,000 as nonrefundable advances on the company performance bonus to be earned pursuant to this section (the "Company Performance Bonus"), paid ratably with the Employee's regular pay (the "Bonus Advance"). The Bonus Advance shall be applied against any Company Performance Bonus earned during 2001. The Executive shall earn annual bonuses as follows:

a. for the year ended December 31, 2001, the Executive shall receive a Company Performance Bonus equal to one percent (1%) of (A) the Company's gross sales for the period starting on the Commencement Date and ending December 31, 2001 (calculated in accordance with generally accepted accounting principles as consistently applied by the Company) less (B) all returns, allowances and discounts applicable to or associated with such gross sales and less (C) any and all amounts paid to third parties for license and application fees (the net value of (A) less (B) and less (C) being referred to as "Company Net Sales");
b. for the year ended December 31, 2002, the Executive shall receive a Company Performance Bonus equal to one percent (1%) of the excess of Company Net Sales for 2002 over Company Net Sales for 2001;

c. for the year ended December 31, 2003, the Executive shall receive a Company Performance Bonus equal to one percent (1%) of the excess of Company Net Sales for 2003 over Company Net Sales for 2002; and
d. for the year ended December 31, 2004, the Executive shall receive a Company Performance Bonus equal to one percent (1%) of the excess of Company Net Sales for 2004 over Company Net Sales for 2003.

Such Company Performance Bonus shall be subject to Section 3.5 herein and shall be payable within ten (10) days after the distribution of the final audited financial statements.

3.3 Quarterly Bonus. For the remainder of 2001, the Executive shall be eligible to receive quarterly bonuses as follows:

a. if the Company achieves Company Net Sales of $234,735 for the fiscal quarter ended June 30, 2001, then the Executive shall receive a quarterly bonus for the second quarter of $5,000;
b. if the Company achieves Company Net Sales of $1,013,905 for the fiscal quarter ended September 30, 2001, then the Executive shall receive a quarterly bonus for the third quarter of $10,000; and
c. if the Company achieves Company Net Sales of $1,278,125 for the fiscal quarter ended December 31, 2001, then the Executive shall receive a quarterly bonus for the fourth quarter of $10,000.
d. Notwithstanding the foregoing, if the Company achieves Company Net Sales of $2,972,210 for the three quarters ending December 31, 2001, but any of the individual quarterly targets were missed, the Executive will nevertheless receive all three quarterly bonuses for 2001, aggregating $25,000.

Such quarterly bonuses shall be payable within thirty (30) days after the end of such fiscal quarter, and shall be subject to Section 3.5 herein. The Executive will be eligible to receive quarterly bonuses, similarly structured as in the 2001 plan, in the years subsequent to 2001. The quarterly bonuses will be structured based on business goals agreed to between the Executive and the Board at the discretion of the Board.

3.4 Annual Bonus. The Executive shall be eligible to receive an annual bonus for each calendar year for which the Company has net income, in an amount equal to fifteen percent (15%) of the net income before taxes, as calculated in accordance with GAAP. Such annual bonus shall be subject to Section 3.5 herein and shall be payable within ten (10) days after the distribution of the final audited financial statements.

Executive's Insight: Signing and Performance Bonuses

Terry Holmes is vice president of sales and marketing for the U.S. branch of a European company. Here, he discusses his experience negotiating a signing and performance bonus. The win–win principles exemplified in this excerpt are shown in the right-hand margin of the text.

"I was recruited for this job about four years ago. Before that, I was director of sales for a technical division of the Polaroid Corporation. I took the position with the understanding that the company would at some stage begin manufacturing somewhere in North America, and at that point I would become general manager/president of that operation.

Principles in Action: Focus on the end goal.

"When I accepted the position, I negotiated for both a signing bonus and a performance bonus. However, I considered the signing bonus far less important than the performance part. The challenge I faced was that I was negotiating with the U.K. division head, when the parent company is Swiss. I have found that the Swiss are very conservative in terms of compensation for individuals. They almost have a rule of thumb where the ratio of the highest salary to the lowest salary in the company would be about thirteen or fourteen to one. This means that the CEO would not make more than fourteen times as much as the lowest-paid employee. The spread is like this in most of Western Europe, but then you come to the United States, and the spread is astronomical—at least that's the way the Swiss look at it. So my intention was to have the performance bonus make up the difference between the salary they would be willing to pay, and the salary I would want to receive.

Principles in Action: Use the bonus to augment your salary.

"In terms of the signing bonus, the salary they were offering me was almost the same as what I was making with Polaroid, so I saw the signing bonus almost as a sign of good faith, a sign that they really wanted me. I brought it up quite early in the process, saying that it was important that the salary be at least commensurate with what I was making, but that the bonus should be greater than my current situation, especially given that I was going into almost a start-up situation. Also, I pointed out that, where they were not offering stock options, they should offer something else in lieu of options—such as a signing bonus.

"As for the performance bonus, my objective was twofold: one, to have a chance for greater earnings, and two, to establish clear performance criteria. The criteria were something like, the company is now doing such-and-such an amount of business; if it doubles, or triples, there should be some appropriate performance bonus tied directly into that. We tied the bonus to objective criteria: the sales and profits of the U.S. subsidiary.

Principles in Action: Insist on using objective criteria.

"At first, they had set forth objectives for year two and year three, with the business essentially doubling by year three. However, during the interview process, it had come out that the subsidiary here in the States had been more or less flat in terms of sales for several years. That, of course, led to some other questions: Why has the subsidiary always been flat? In your estimation, why hasn't the business grown? And those questions led into some other issues: the services and products the company offers are on a long sales cycle, typically two years, and the company had pretty substantial turnover. So if it took employees two or three years to catch on to what the company can and cannot do, but the employees turned over every three to four years, then the key seemed clear: We needed to figure out ways to keep people motivated and to keep them with the company for a longer period of time.

"At the same time, in terms of the performance bonus, I pointed out that their numbers didn't add up. Their sales had been flat for ten years, they had been unprofitable for at least that long; now I was coming on board, not knowing much about the company, and they were looking to double the business by year three. I insisted that they agree to revisit the numbers each year, and they did.

Principles in Action: Make sure the goals are realistic and achievable.

"Of course, before that, I had confirmed that sales really had been flat for that long. First, I asked if I could speak to the company controller, and to one of their current employees over here. They knew that I was interested in them, and I was their leading candidate at that point, so they agreed to that. I met with one of their senior people here; then, when I went to the U.K. for a final interview in front of their directors, I pulled the controller aside and had a thirty-minute discussion with him, in which he confirmed some of these things.

Principles in Action: Know the company.

"After I had collected that information, I put together a proposal for my compensation. I put together a formal letter, including the reasons why I felt that compensation was appropriate, and sent them a copy in advance. Then their sales director came over here, having reviewed everything, and we met to finalize the deal. Essentially, we talked about a couple of fairly insignificant points, then shook hands and agreed to a start date.

"In preparation for negotiating a bonus, I would say, start by understanding the industry. Try to get some perspective on whether there is anything unique in regard to compensation for people in this industry. I think one of the smartest things I did in preparing to negotiate was to speak to the controller and to a long-term employee. Don't be afraid to get advice from others. If you know someone in a higher management position than you, ask them for advice. It never hurts to get a second opinion. And be up front. If you believe that you are one of the leading candidates, make sure that you get all the compensation information out on the table, whether it's what you are looking for or what they are seeking."

Principles in Action: Know the industry.

Chapter Summary: Signing and Performance Bonuses

- **Average signing bonuses.** The average is 5 to 10 percent of base salary, depending on the position and industry, but it's not uncommon for top executives to command up to 25 percent of their base salaries.
- **Build your case in advance.** Determine your requirements; establish objective criteria in terms of bonuses for similar positions in your industry.
- **Identify objective milestones and get the specifics in writing.** Attempt to identify specific objective milestones, not subjective ones, and make sure your employment agreement includes both the bonus achievement dates and how and when you get paid.
- **Use bonuses as a way to invent options for mutual gain.** If you can't reach agreement on your desired base salary, suggest a creative bonus structure, based on performance, to reach your overall compensation goals.
- **Plan for taxes.** Bonuses are treated as compensation for income tax purposes.
- **Be aware of payback clauses.** Employers frequently require employees to pay back a signing bonus if the employee voluntarily terminates his or her employment before a certain time.

CHAPTER SEVEN

Benefits

I took a good look at what I needed, what I could and couldn't do without, so there was an area for compromise rather than all my way or no way.

—Terri Pla
VP, Sales and Business Development

◆ The Challenge and Overview

All employers offer their employees wages. Most also offer other benefits, some fully paid, some subsidized, and some that the employee must pay for. The benefits offered vary widely from company to company, and can even vary within a company, depending on the employee's place within the company hierarchy and how badly the company wants to gain the employee's services. By and large, benefits fall into several broad categories:

- Stock options
- Retirement plans, including company-paid plans and employee-paid plans
- Insurance, including health, life, and disability
- Paid time off, including holidays, vacation, sick time, sympathetic leave
- Transportation, including a company car, company-sponsored van pool, transit pass, paid parking
- Miscellaneous, including tuition reimbursement, fitness/health club plans, child care allowance, flexible scheduling, and telecommuting

Some companies offer the same benefits plan to all employees. Others offer cafeteria plans, where employees can choose from a variety of options, some paid for by the company, some merely made available to employees, who must pay for the benefits themselves. Many cafeteria plans include the option of having money deducted from pretax income to pay for such qualified benefits as medical and dental insurance. Employees can also choose to pay for other, nonqualified, benefits with after-tax dollars.

Using these plans, employees save on their income taxes because contributing money for fringe benefits reduces their pretax income. Employers like the plans because they don't have to pay FICA taxes on the income allocated to the plan. Such plans also enable employers to provide a wider variety of benefits without necessarily incurring the higher costs associated with them. They may simply pass on the costs to employees who pay for the benefits with pretax income.

If you're being offered fringe benefits through a flexible benefits plan or cafeteria plan, be sure to find out exactly what the employer is paying for and what you're expected to contribute toward the benefits. Some employers may present a list of benefits available under the cafeteria plan, but do not actually contribute financially toward providing the benefits for employees. Know what the employer is going to pay and what you're going to have to pay to obtain these fringe benefits.

While the value of fringe benefits is not always readily apparent, because there may be no monetary amount assigned to them, their value is real. Benefits and perks can be worth 30 to 40 percent of your base salary, although the percentage varies considerably depending on the specific benefits being offered. Negotiating for such benefits as having the employer pay the full health insurance premium is a way to indirectly negotiate more pay. When comparing job offers, the value of fringe benefits must be included to determine which offer provides more value to the employee.

It is important to understand the tax implications of certain fringe benefits. Some benefits, such as moving/relocation expenses and car allowances, are taxable as non-wage compensation; others, such as health insurance or qualified employee discounts, are not. While a relocation package or car allowance may seem like a generous benefit, if you don't take into account the potential tax implications, you could end up with a significantly smaller benefit than you anticipated.

◆ Preparation

Benefits packages at a framework level are often standard; however, there is room for negotiation. Start by compiling an overview list of what is important to you, for example, time off, personal days, fully subsidized health coverage, car allowance, day care subsidies, fitness plan, life insurance, AD&D insurance (accidental death and dismemberment), and retirement plans. Once you've compiled your list, annotate it, briefly stating why each item is important to you. Going through this process in advance will help you negotiate more effectively. Also, you may wish to use this list as a point of reference during the actual discussion; even if you don't get all the benefits you desire, your preparedness makes a favorable impression on the employer. Your list of benefits can also be used as a negotiating strategy in other areas of your overall package. If you get turned down on a few key benefits, you may be able to use this to persuade the employer to compromise in other areas.

◆ The Negotiation

Different companies offer different benefits. Some are willing to negotiate on benefits, and some are not. If certain benefits are important to you, identify them in advance. Make sure you are able to articulate their importance to you. Also, be prepared to point out their indirect value to the company, as they will contribute to your performance by alleviating other pressures. At the same time, keep in mind the risks of making any element of the negotiation personal.

We've prepared a comprehensive list of questions to ask yourself before engaging in the discussion process. Choose carefully which elements to negotiate for. If you focus too closely on any one small issue, you run the risk of winning the battle in terms of a small benefit negotiation and losing the war with regard to the value of your overall compensation package.

Analysis

Analyze the situation, your interests, and those of the other party, and begin gathering information. You will need to develop answers to questions like these:

Key Questions

- What benefits am I currently receiving?
- Which of these benefits do I value most?
- Where would I place my priorities in terms of benefits—flexibility/variety of offerings, financial security/retirement planning, time off, insurance, family-oriented benefits, etc.?
- Is any one benefit so important to me that I would refuse the job if the company couldn't offer it?
- How would I quantify intangible benefits (e.g., celebrating birthdays, company-provided lunches, flexible schedules, etc.)?

Planning

Use planning to establish your strategy, understand the other party's interests, and determine what options or alternatives would be acceptable outcomes. Ask yourself questions like these as part of your planning process:

Key Questions

- Which benefits, if any, are negotiable?
- How will I present the benefits that are most important to me?
- What objective criteria have I collected on the benefits employers commonly offer?
- What are the employer's interests (e.g., standardization of benefits, providing a variety of benefits to recruit key employees, minimizing costs)?
- Are my health providers covered by the company's insurance plan, or would I need to change providers to join the plan?

Discussion

During the negotiation, you can collect new information in two ways: through questions you ask the interviewer, and through unsolicited information the interviewer shares as part of the discussion. These are some of the questions you should ask and information you should listen for:

Questions to Ask

- What is the company's benefits package?
- Is there a cafeteria plan? What is included?
- Which benefits does the company pay for, and which do employees pay for?
- Are any of these benefits negotiable (e.g., start date for health insurance or number of vacation days)?
- If I am not interested in a specific benefit, but would like another one that is not included in the standard package, is an exchange possible?
- How long would I have to wait for benefits to begin? Health insurance? 401(k)? Profit sharing? Other retirement funds? Tuition reimbursement?

Health Insurance

- Can you describe the company's health insurance plan? What are the different choices offered? Dental coverage? Vision coverage?
- Has the company recently changed insurance providers, or are there plans to change in the next enrollment cycle?
- What is the co-pay for medical insurance? How much is the employee responsible for paying?

401(k) or Profit Sharing Plans

- Do you have a 401(k) or profit sharing plan?
- Does the company make any contributions to the 401(k) plan? If so, how much is the contribution?
- Can you describe the profit sharing plan and the percentage allocated for employee participation?

- How are the profits determined on an individual basis? Is it equal distribution or pro rata depending upon an employee's role or salary level within the company?

Paid Time Off

- How is paid time off handled—in a single PTO (paid time off) account or with separate sick and vacation time?
- What are the sick leave policy and procedures?
- Can I take unpaid time off in addition to paid time off?
- What is the vacation accrual schedule?
- Can vacation and/or sick days be carried from one calendar year to the next?
- Does the company offer a sabbatical program? (After a set period of employment, an employee may take a number of weeks/months for personal enrichment, study, or other pursuit.)

Other Benefits

- Is flex time (working flexible hours) an option?
- What is the telecommuting policy?
- Does the company offer any health club subsidies or benefits?
- What is the maternity/paternity leave policy?
- Is the company large enough to be covered by the Family and Medical Leave Act (FMLA), which enables an employee to take up to twelve weeks of unpaid leave to care for a newborn or newly adopted child or family member who is ill? (Smaller employers are not subject to the same requirements.)
- Does the company offer on-site child care or have a contract with a child care provider for reduced rates for company employees?
- Does the company offer car payment subsidies? If so, what are the requirements for such a subsidy—that the car is used primarily for sales calls, that the employee is

required to travel extensively, or is it an executive benefit, with no other eligibility criteria?

- Does the company offer tuition reimbursement or other tangible support for continuing education?
- Does the company hold an annual (or more frequent) all-company event for fun, information sharing, and community building (e.g., holiday party, quarterly meeting, etc.)?
- Is there a casual dress policy?

Information to Listen For

- Does the company "walk the walk" when it comes to delivering benefits and using benefits to attract and retain employees?

◆ Outcome: Next Steps

Once you understand the scope of the benefits offered, make sure those benefits are included in the framework of your employment agreement. The benefits section of an executive's employee agreement that follows is divided into fringe benefits, vacation, reimbursement of expenses, and health insurance. Each of these areas must be explicitly stated to avoid ambiguity when you begin your new position.

One way to gauge the company's attitude toward its employees is to ask to see a copy of the employee manual. The manual should be about ten to fifteen pages long; its purpose is to reflect the company's culture, ethics, and policies. If the company does not have an employee manual, or does not wish to let you see it, this should raise a red flag. It may mean that the company is not well managed or organized. The manual will also give you information about the way the company treats employees.

A review of the employee manual will also answer many of your questions about benefits without your needing to ask the interviewer. Asking such questions at an early stage of the process may make you appear too focused on "What am I getting out of this?" rather than "How can I contribute?"

When asking for a copy of the employee manual, you might say something like, "I'm comfortable with the people, the job seems interesting; as the last part of my information-gathering process, I'd like to review your employee manual, rather than our going into all the details now. Since these will be the guidelines that govern my relationship with the company, I'd like to be clear on your policies and procedures before I make a long-term commitment to the company."

The fringe benefits section is basic in this excerpt; this section should include car allowance, day care subsidies, health club, or any other perk that has been negotiated on your behalf.

The second section, vacation time, outlines time off. Many executives negotiate additional vacation time. For example, if the company policy is two weeks paid the first year, you might negotiate to receive four weeks off, with one additional week paid and the second additional week unpaid.

The third section is reimbursement of expenses. Again, it is important to clearly state the company's policy with regard to reimbursing expenses. When there is no defined policy, it's important to define, in writing, a clear process for requesting reimbursement for expenses. The agreement should state that upon submitting expenses, you will be reimbursed within ten or fifteen business days. This section may include a clause stating a maximum amount that an executive may incur without prior approval from the CEO. Clauses like this are used to maintain tight fiscal controls—a sign that the company places a value on its cash flow and expenses.

Health insurance is the fourth key subsection under the benefits section. This section should clearly state what the executive will receive with respect to health benefits. Many companies have co-pay programs, where the company will subsidize a percentage of the premium. However, with executives, a company may pay the full premium as an added benefit, rather than increasing the executive's salary. This is an advantage to the company because they can deduct this benefit as an expense, which is not subject to payroll taxes. It is also, of course, a significant benefit to the executive and his or her family, and is a way to indirectly negotiate more pay.

Example as Excerpted from an Executive's Employment Agreement

3.8 Fringe Benefits. The Executive shall be entitled to participate in all benefit programs that the Company establishes and makes available to its employees, if any.

3.9 Vacation. The Executive shall be allowed three (3) weeks of paid vacation during each calendar year.

3.10 Reimbursement of Expenses. The Company shall reimburse the Executive for all normal business expenses incurred or paid by the Executive in connection with, or related to, the performance of his or her duties, responsibilities or services under this Agreement, upon presentation by the Executive of documentation, expense statements, vouchers or such other supporting information as the Company may reasonably request.

3.11 Health Insurance. For so long as the Company has an established health care plan, the Company shall pay one hundred percent (100%) of the premium for the Executive's participation in the Company's health care plan, such that the Executive and all members of his or her family are provided health care coverage under the plan.

Executive's Insight: Benefits

Terri Pla began her career in medical sales, then moved into strategic sales consulting for IT companies. She is currently vice president of sales and business development focusing on sales strategy and infrastructure for emerging growth companies. The win–win principles exemplified in this excerpt are shown in the right-hand margin of the text.

"When you negotiate benefits with a new employer, obviously, the first thing you look at is the financial package, but apart from that, it's important to take a good look at anything the company offers, or could potentially offer, even if they haven't up to that point. If they don't have a 401(k) program in place, they should at least be looking toward implementing a program to help people attain financial security down the line.

"One of the challenges with negotiating a benefits package is that you want to keep the level of benefits you have already achieved. For example, once your vacation time has risen to a certain level—say, three or four weeks a year—you're not going to want to start with a new organization at two weeks vacation and build that up again. However, many companies have a set policy for their vacation plans, which might not match with your expectations. From the company's point of view, you are a new hire; the time you built up was not built up with them. Also, when you are just coming in, the company doesn't like to hear right up front that you want to take a certain amount of time. Then again, if the company respects you, they will at least be open to discussing the topic. Keep in mind that both parties have goals, and you should be able to come to a compromise that works for both sides.

Principles in Action: Identify your interests.

"At one stage, my vacation benefits were up to four weeks a year, and I went into an organization where the offer was one week during the first year, two weeks after that, and three weeks after five years. That was the company's standard, but it was just not acceptable for me. So I talked with the person I was negotiating with and said, 'This is something I worked toward for a long time. With this amount of time built up, it would be a huge problem for me to take a step back and say this is OK with me because it's OK with everyone else.' Ultimately, we were able to work something out. I received three weeks in the first year, and four weeks after that. Under some circumstances, even corporate standards may be flexible.

"Sometimes this is made more difficult by the company structure. If you're discussing things with a hiring manager, that person may not have the authority to adjust things like vacation time. Some people are tempted to say, 'Why don't you let me talk directly with so-and-so,' meaning the person with the authority, but in the long run, that isn't very effective, either. If you're going to be working with the person doing the hiring, you don't want to start out by sidestepping them. A more constructive approach would be to say something like, 'So that everything is covered from all angles, can all

Principles in Action: Invent options for mutual gain.

three of us meet together so we can make sure we're all on the same page?' That way, you have the dialogue with both the hiring manager and the person who has the authority, without offending anyone.

"When you start negotiating benefits, you need to look at the big picture, and take into account all the information you have. For example, in one case, I found the opportunity myself rather than going through a headhunter. Knowing that the company was not obligated to make a sizable payment to someone else for finding me, I was able to negotiate an appropriate signing bonus. However, there will be other instances where that wouldn't be an appropriate request to make. It's a matter of being sensitive to the company. Rather than starting with something that they will find too difficult to accept, go with something that makes sense. And in that case, a signing bonus made sense. Another time, I had had a company car for a number of years, then moved to a job that didn't offer a car. Since I was in a sales position, I needed a car for work on a daily basis, so I negotiated to have the company lease a car for me. Again, that was reasonable for that particular position. If I were in something like an IT position, where I needed to be in one location at all times, that is probably not something I would request. Focus on what will appear reasonable to the company as well as to you, and you should be able to come to a reasonable solution.

Principles in Action: Identify the company's needs.

"When I negotiated the car lease, the biggest challenge was that this wasn't something the company had done before. A lot of people find that daunting; they aren't comfortable with that. But you know, someone always has to be the first, so why not you? If it's something that you are accustomed to, or that would be required for the job, and that the company is capable of doing, then you can present yourself with confidence and make a case. It just has to be something that makes sense. You should be able to present it to the company as, 'When this makes sense for me, it makes sense for you.'

"After salary and a signing bonus, I think the next benefits I would look for would be stock options and ownership. Then would come vacation time, and things like a car or car payment. I usually negotiate to have the company provide me with a home office. It's important for me to be able to get work done whenever and however I see fit, whether that is in an office or in a dedicated area in my home. If I know that I want to work in that environment rather than in an office, and that it's just as effective, then that's one of the things I will negotiate. Again, there have been times when I was the first person who had ever made that request, but I used my talent and my ability as a negotiating point. I made sure that the person I was negotiating with was aware of all the benefits of having me work for them, so they didn't perceive me as saying 'This is what I want,' they saw me as saying 'This is what I need in order to do what you want me to do very, very well.'

Principles in Action: Prioritize your needs.

"To prepare for the negotiation, I took a good look at what I needed, what I could and couldn't do without. That way, there's an area for compromise rather than 'my way or no way.' I listed my abilities and the company's needs, where the things I wanted to negotiate on were or were not relevant to my capabilities and their needs. I also listed the things that were a bonus, in a way, things that were not necessary but that I would want in order to be in that place, things that were important to me. By preparing in advance, I knew before talking to them what things I would bend on or let go of, and what things I would not.

Principles in Action: Identify your needs.

"When you are looking at a company's benefits package, you can really divide it into several main areas: compensation; security, in terms of health insurance and retirement plans; and time to be able to do whatever else you need to be able to do. Those things are really important. Even if a company can't negotiate in other areas, they should be willing to negotiate in these.

"The most important thing is to keep in mind what makes sense and what doesn't, what is reasonable, what is fair for both sides. I would not personally try to negotiate for something that didn't make sense for the employer. But if something is important to me, then I would be pretty firm on that to get whatever it is that I need, and let some of the other things work themselves out in other ways.

Principles in Action: Make the discussion a win–win process.

Use your strengths as a position to negotiate from, but do what's fair. Don't let go of the things that are most important to you, because being happy day to day is critical. If you look at things from the company's perspective as well as your own, then you get what you need, and they get what they need to keep the business flourishing. It's win–win. And when it's all done with a focus on fairness to both sides, there are no lingering hard feelings from the side that had to compromise and accept something they didn't want to."

Chapter Summary: Benefits

- **Prioritize the benefits that are important to you.** Benefits vary from company to company, and fall into several broad categories: insurance, paid time off, transportation, retirement plans, profit sharing plans, miscellaneous (tuition reimbursement, fitness, child care allowance, telecommuting). Identify the ones that are most important to you.
- **Benefits are standard, but there is room for negotiation.** Prepare a list of what's important to you and why, and use this as a basis for a discussion when negotiating benefits.
- **Use benefits to negotiate other areas of your employment agreement**. If you get turned down on a few key benefits, use this to persuade the employer to compromise in other areas.
- **Understand the tax impact of certain benefits.** Some benefits, such as car allowance, are taxable as non-wage compensation, so plan accordingly.
- **Get everything in writing.** Clearly specify in writing all benefits, such as expense reimbursement procedures and time frame, vacation time, and health insurance.

CHAPTER EIGHT

Relocation

> *Sit down and look at your current monthly expenses, and make sure you have a firm understanding of exactly what those same categories are going to cost you on the other end. Your cost of living increase is different from my cost of living increase, because we are different people, we have different lives.*
>
> —Carla Washinko, CFO

◆ The Challenge and Overview

Accepting a new job often involves moving to a new area. Relocating for a new job can offer a number of benefits, but there are also challenges. In a new location, you must start from scratch to build a network of contacts, both professional and social. If you have children, changing schools can be a difficult adjustment. Before considering relocation, you need to evaluate the costs and benefits of the move for all aspects of your life.

Once you have made the decision to relocate, it is in your best interest to make sure that your new employer covers the financial costs of your relocation. A major move can mean many adjustments; it doesn't have to mean incurring major costs. Most employers (especially medium- and large-sized companies) will pay an employee's moving expenses and even help the new employee find housing in the new city. The easiest way to calculate relocation expenses, and to make cost-of-living comparisons, is to use an on-line calculator. (To find one, search for "cost-of-living calculator.")

You will want to determine which moving-related expenses your employer covers and negotiate the amount to be covered prior to accepting the job. If possible, this should be kept separate from a signing bonus, which might be received for accepting the job offer.

Keep in mind that payment of relocation expenses is considered taxable income for you as an employee. Consequently, for someone in the 31 percent tax bracket, a $3,000 relocation package would be worth just over $2,000 after taxes. When negotiating for a relocation package, it's wise to start with the dollar amount you need to have for the relocation. Then add on a percentage of that amount to cover the income taxes.

> ***Example:*** Joanne MacDonald was offered a senior management position that would require her to move from Washington, D.C. to Denver, Colorado. In the initial job offer, the new employer offered to reimburse Joanne for $1,500 in relocation expenses. Joanne almost accepted the offer; her research regarding moving costs and the cost of living in Denver suggested that this would cover her expenses. However, further research showed Joanne that the reimbursement would be taxable income and that close to one-third of the $1,500 reimbursement would be required to pay the income taxes. Joanne needed to have $1,500 in take-home pay to cover the relocation. She presented a counteroffer to the employer, requesting $2,100 for relocation and explaining that, because of the tax implications, $1,500 would not cover the relocation expenses. By substantiating her position with research and a clear explanation for her reasoning, Joanne was able to persuade the new employer to increase the relocation reimbursement.

◆ Preparation

If you are interviewing for a position that would require you to move, it is usually expected that the company will reimburse you for your relocation expenses. However, although this is typical, you should not assume anything; this must be addressed early in the negotiations process. The specific terms can be addressed later, once salary and compensation issues have been clarified.

In the preparation stage, it is important to take the time to project your moving expenses. This can involve obtaining accurate information on moving companies, getting quotes, projecting any loss you may incur if you need to sell your house, determining living expenses while in transition, moving your family, and other ancillary costs associated with any move. You should carefully anticipate and project all your expenses in order to negotiate this component of your employment agreement. Calculating all expenses and compiling a line-item list of what you anticipate will provide a framework for your negotiations. If you are candid with the employer, showing your thought process and related expenses, you will often engender respect rather than resentment.

◆ The Negotiation

Now you're ready to negotiate your relocation package. This is often a fairly straightforward discussion process. Your expenses are what they are, and if the company wants you, they will often accommodate your needs. It's important to do your homework and plan thoroughly here, because companies will not give you a blank check. You should anticipate extraordinary expenses that would not have occurred if you had not been required to move. We've delineated some of the key areas that you might want to explore before engaging in the discussion process.

Analysis

Consider your own interests, and those of the other party, by doing a self-analysis and an opportunity analysis. You will need to develop answers to questions like these:

Key Questions

Self-Analysis

- How do I feel about moving?
- How does my spouse/partner/family feel about relocating?
- What time frame am I comfortable with for this move?

Opportunity Analysis

- Will the employer provide spouse employment assistance

(often available through outplacement companies)?

- Will the employer provide help to find schools for my children?
- Can the employer introduce me to people (employees or community members) with similar interests?

Planning

Use planning to establish your strategy, understand the other party's interests, and determine what options or alternatives would be acceptable outcomes. Ask yourself questions like these as part of your planning process:

Key Questions

- What is the employer's interest in having me relocate?
- Are there any options other than relocation?
- What is the level of urgency from the employer's perspective?
- How would I prefer to receive the relocation funds—as an up-front lump sum (based on estimated expenses) or as a reimbursement of expenses actually incurred?
- Have I considered all relocation expenses, including installation fees for services such as phone, cable, and gas?

Discussion

During the negotiation, these are some of the questions you should ask:

Questions to Ask

- Are you going to pay a lump sum or actual reimbursement of costs incurred?
- What's the turnaround for paying expenses?
- What is your policy for reimbursement? How does it work?
- Will you purchase my house if I can't sell it?

- Will you pay to locate and rent an executive apartment for several months while I acclimate to the area?
- What provisions will you make to return me to my home location if this arrangement is not mutually successful?
- Does the company include a requirement that the employee refund the relocation costs if he or she leaves the company within a certain period of time?

◆ Outcome: Next Steps

Once you've negotiated your relocation reimbursement terms, it is important to get everything in writing. It's not enough to say, in an employment agreement or offer letter, that "the company will reimburse for moving expenses"; such a statement is not specific enough. The agreement should explicitly state what expenses will be reimbursed (i.e., executive apartment rental, closing costs on your house, apartment search fees, actual moving costs, etc.), the procedure for submitting expenses, and the time frame for reimbursement once expenses are submitted. This is all standard language that you should look for in the relocation reimbursement clause of your employment agreement or offer letter.

In the following example, all these issues were covered clearly and concisely. It's an excellent example of how various issues are covered, such as an executive apartment rental and closing costs on a house.

Example as Excerpted from an Executive's Employment Agreement

Relocation Allowance. The Company agrees to provide the Executive with a Relocation Allowance which will not exceed $10,000. The purpose for this Relocation Allowance is to reimburse the Executive for relocation expenses actually incurred. As such, the Executive shall be required to provide the Company with copies of receipts for all relocation expenses incurred. The Company shall reimburse the Executive for all such relocation expenses within fifteen (15) days of receipt of each receipt. For the purposes of this provision, relocation expenses shall include actual moving, packing, and unpacking expenses for all household goods and automobiles, expenses incurred in the sale of your home, including sales commissions and closing costs, expenses incurred in the purchase of a new home, including closing costs, and temporary housing costs for a period of no longer than ____ weeks.

Executive's Insight: Relocation

Carla Washinko is chief financial officer of a 220-employee company. Her former employer was a large public accounting firm with offices around the United States and in Europe. The win–win principles exemplified in this excerpt are shown in the right-hand margin of the text.

"I actually started with the company in the Washington, D.C. office, right out of school. I had been working with them for about five years when I saw a notice in an internal publication for a temporary position in New York. It sounded interesting, so I applied for the position, and was accepted. So the relocation was essentially a part of that, moving from Washington D.C. to the New York City office.

"Now, at the time, as I said, I had been out of school for about five years, so I was really still quite naive. I had never moved anywhere with a company before. The relocation package was raised with me by my new supervisor. Essentially, the terms of the move were dictated to me. They agreed to pay for the cost of moving, the cost of coming to New York to look for a place to live, meals and expenses during those searches, and the commission on the sale of my house.

"They also agreed to pay the cost of my buying another home when I returned to D.C., in terms of paying the settlement costs—inspection, assessment, all that. They said they wouldn't pay points, obviously, buying down the rate, but they paid all the other costs of settlement.

"They offered all that up front. At the same time, they ask all employees to sign a note for a reimbursement for moving expenses that is forgiven over the period of time that you're in the temporary assignment. So, for example, if you go to London for a twenty-four-month assignment, and your moving expenses are $30,000, you sign a note that says you will continue to work for the company for the entire twenty-four-month period of your temporary assignment. Over the course of the twenty-four months, the $30,000 is forgiven, at a rate of about $1,250 a month. If you leave before the twenty-four months are up, you need to repay the company for whatever balance is remaining. So if you left after fourteen months, $17,500 of the $30,000 would have been forgiven, but you would have to repay the company the remaining $12,500. The whole relocation package was a written agreement between myself and the company.

"But there were a lot of other things that I was too inexperienced to even raise as issues. For example, when I left D.C., one of the decisions I made was to get rid of my car, because having a car in New York is so expensive. Had I been a better negotiator at the time, or just more experienced, I might have raised that issue and made that a part of the negotiation. I just assumed that the sensible thing to do would be to sell my car, and buy a new one when I moved back. But then, two years later, I was going to have to buy a new car, whereas if I had stayed in D.C., I probably would not have been buying a new car. If I had had more experience, I might have asked the company to pay for garaging my car in New York, and to cover the increase in insurance from D.C. to New York.

"Also, as I talked to other people, I realized that there were other things I could have negotiated. For example, one of the men I was working with had come to New York from Atlanta, also on a temporary assignment. Since his apartment in New York was much smaller than his house in Atlanta, he had the company pay for storage for most of his stuff in Atlanta. I hadn't been aware that this was a possibility, so I had gotten rid of a lot of things. Of course, I was only four years out of college, so my things were what my mother used to call 'early American garage sale,' but if I had been better educated on different negotiable aspects of a move, I probably would have wanted to store them, not get rid of them.

"Another factor I didn't take into account was the change to my salary. At the time, most major accounting firms paid overtime, so I actually made about 50 percent above my base in overtime. In D.C., I had a base of $35,000, so with overtime, I was actually earning close to $50,000. With the New York move, my base went from $35,000 to $60,000. Looking only at the base salary, the increase was pretty significant. But in New York, I had quite a bit less overtime. So we're looking at a real increase from $50,000 to $60,000. That essentially covered some of the cost-of-living issues; of course, rents in New York are significantly higher than in Washington. But I was not aware of the change in tax structure. I didn't realize that there was a New York City tax as well as the state tax. That made quite a difference to my net income.

"However, my second relocation—with the same company—was much better, because I knew I had the opportunity to negotiate some of these things. Also, this time, the move was at the company's request. By this time, I was back in the Washington office, a few years after my temporary New York assignment. The company wanted to export some of the experience we had in the D.C. office to some of their other offices, so they asked two of us to move to other offices. They gave me a choice of San Jose or Philadelphia. I did some basic research on both cost of living in different regions and the salaries that the managers in those offices were making compared to what I was making in D.C, so I could get a ballpark range of what I could expect to negotiate for myself. Interestingly enough, the managers in the different offices of a major accounting firm don't earn appreciably different salaries, no matter where they are—whether in San Francisco or in Kansas. Now, in Kansas, you could get a small three-bedroom house for about $100,000. In Washington, it would be about $180,000. But in San Francisco, it would be about $400,000 for the same house. The San Francisco managers weren't making significantly more than the managers in the Philadelphia office, and I expected that my compensation would be kept to the range that was the norm in those offices. That was a large part of my decision to stay on the East Coast, and not move to California.

Principles in Action: Research in advance.

"When it came to negotiating the relocation package, I felt that I was in a much stronger position. First of all, of course, this was a move they wanted me to make, as opposed to something that I was requesting. I also had a lot more knowledge

Principles in Action: Identify the company's interests.

about the possibilities, having talked to lots of people in the intervening years. I don't have any regrets about that move, no feelings of 'Gee, I wish I had negotiated for such-and-such.'

"Essentially, the company paid all my moving expenses, and gave me a pretty significant salary increase—about 25 percent. There was certainly some negotiation involved in that. One of the things I did in preparation for this move that I had not done in the New York negotiation was get a lot of information on cost of living in every major expenditure category. *The Wall Street Journal* has a fair number of statistics available for purchase. When I sat down with the managing partner in Philadelphia, he started telling me how much lower the cost of living is in Philly than in D.C. In terms of housing prices, that is true. If you use 100 as the average housing price in the United States, Washington is about 140, and at that time, Philadelphia was about 120. Because I had done my research, I was able to say, 'Yes, you're right when it comes to housing, but most of the other cost categories are much higher in Philadelphia—food, heating, utilities, clothing, gasoline, the tax structure.' I was better prepared to be able to counter his arguments. He had wanted me to move at the same salary, but I negotiated a 25 percent salary increase.

Principles in Action: Establish objective criteria.

"On top of that, I asked for a pretty basic package: reimbursement for the cost of selling my home in Virginia again, reimbursement for the house-hunting trips, reimbursement for the cost to buy a home here, temporary living expenses until I found a home here, the cost of the movers. The whole thing came to about $30,000.

"One difference between these two negotiations was certainly the amount of knowledge I went into the negotiation with. Another was my level within the company. In the first negotiation, I was the lowly accounting senior, whereas in the second I was a senior manager. Also, I had worked with the managing partner while he was in the D.C. office, so I knew his personality, I knew how much I could push him. Although there was still a hierarchical relationship—he was a managing partner, and I was only a manager, not a partner—it was more a peer relationship in terms of familiarity level. That level of familiarity allowed me to push a little more than I might have otherwise. For example, when we were discussing salary, he said, 'Look, I lived in Washington, housing is a lot more expensive there. You are moving to a much less expensive area, there's no reason to increase your salary.' My familiarity with him made it easier to go back and forth with him over that, which I might not have done with someone with whom I had had no previous professional relationship.

Principles in Action: Communicate clearly.

"Overall, when negotiating a relocation package, you need to understand the true cost of items that are important to you. For example, when I moved to New York, I didn't have children. Another employee, who moved there from Salt Lake City, had four children. He told me later that one thing he should have considered in his negotiation was child care expenses. He had looked at the major categories of expenses—food, money, clothing, utilities, housing, transportation. He didn't calculate the cost of child care, but it was a pretty significant increase. My advice to anyone looking at relocation would be to sit down and look at your current monthly expenses, and make sure you have a firm understanding of exactly what those same categories are going to cost you on the other end. Because your cost of living increase is different from my cost of living increase, because we are different people, we have different lives."

Principles in Action: Prioritize your needs.

Chapter Summary: Relocation

- **Make a list of your anticipated moving expenses.** Negotiate which moving expenses are covered prior to accepting a job. Collect objective data from moving companies or apartment rental agencies.
- **Anticipate ancillary moving expenses.** Consider executive apartment rental, closing costs on your home, apartment search fees, and car transportation costs.

- **Relocation expenses are considered taxable income.** Keep in mind that if you anticipate needing $5,000 for your move and you're in the 31 percent tax bracket, you'll need to negotiate for $7,250 to cover your moving expenses and associated taxes.
- **Get everything in writing.** Clearly understand the company's reimbursement policy and specify the time frame in your employment agreement or offer letter.

CHAPTER NINE

Nondisclosure/Nonsolicitation/ Noncompete Agreement

Focus on the relationship; don't let the negotiation ruin the relationship coming in, because that's the most important thing.

—Randy Grigg, Managing Director

◆ The Challenge and Overview

A *nondisclosure agreement* is an agreement to keep all proprietary information of the employer and the employer's customers and clients confidential. It prohibits the executive from using any of this confidential information for any purpose other than furthering the business goals and objectives of the employer. Confidential information includes customer lists, price lists, and company and client financial information as well as marketing plans and strategies. Even if there is no formal nondisclosure agreement protecting an employer's confidential information, most jurisdictions have laws prohibiting an employee from using confidential information for purposes that benefit any employer other than the owner of the confidential information. The higher an executive rises in a company, the more this becomes an issue, as he or she is exposed to more information that could jeopardize the competitive advantage of the employer. Nondisclosure agreements may also be required early in the interviewing process, before the company will share detailed internal information with the interviewee.

A *nonsolicitation agreement* is designed to prevent the executive, for a specified period after he or she leaves the company, from hiring any person who was an employee with the company and from soliciting any of the company's current customers, clients, and near-term prospects. Under the terms of such an agreement, the executive is allowed to work for the competition. Nonsolicitation agreements should be considered a strong alternative to a noncompete agreement.

A *noncompete agreement,* or "covenant not to compete" clause, as it is commonly called, is essentially a promise by the executive not to compete with his or her employer for a specified period of time in a particular segment of the marketplace. A noncompete agreement can be seen as a separate agreement or as a clause within the employment contract.

Nondisclosure, nonsolicitation, and noncompete agreements may be negotiated as a stand-alone contract or as part of a broader employment agreement involving noncompete, nonsolicitation, and assignment of inventions provisions. They should be carefully negotiated or evaluated by an employment attorney before signing.

The noncompete agreement is the element that poses the greatest challenge. If you sign too restrictive an agreement, you might find yourself restricted from ever working in your area of expertise if you are laid off or terminated. It's important to have a thorough understanding of what you're signing.

Like most things, such agreements really depend on which side of the issue you're on. As an employer, you want to protect intellectual property and to ensure that no one working for you will share your information with a competitor. As an employee, you want to keep your options as wide open as possible so that if you have to leave the company you're not limited in terms of making a living. These two vantage points can seem to be in opposition to each other.

Example: Alex Benito, an associate attorney at a small law firm, decided to leave the practice after three years. The senior partner, Dan Morrison, expected him to practice law, but not to call his clients and say, "We've had a great time working for you and I really did 90 percent of the work. I'd like to continue our relationship; however, I've recently switched to another firm." This is the core issue companies are looking to prevent: stealing clients and stealing customers. Dan believed that it was not reasonable to prevent any ex-employee from practicing law, but believed that it was both reasonable and required that his employees not actively recruit the firm's clients upon departure. By clearly understanding his own objectives and balancing them with Alex's right to make a living in his industry, Dan offered a nonsolicitation agreement as an alternative to a noncompetition agreement, because it protected his firm's primary interests.

Looking through a legal lens, the covenants need to be reasonable in order to be enforceable. The agreements must be limited in both scope and duration. Generally, noncompete agreements that are two years or less in length, and are not overly broad in terms of geographic scope, will be upheld. Similarly, noncompete agreements must be restricted to actual competition and may not be so broad as to prevent earning a living. For example, a covenant stating that an employee working in the software industry in Chicago who left the company would be restricted from working anywhere in the industry for twenty years would be far too restrictive. It would be viewed by the courts as unenforceable. However, an agreement that the employee could not work in the software industry in the Chicago area for eighteen months would probably be seen as reasonable.

It is important to remember that, in a conflict between an individual and a corporation, the individual is at an immediate disadvantage. You may believe that a document is unenforceable, but if an employer wants to pursue legal action against you, they can use corporate assets to fund the litigation, while you will need to use personal assets. Even if you feel that the demands being imposed on you are unrealistic, challenging those demands can be difficult. The best time to address the issue is before you take the job.

In order to be valid, noncompete contracts must be entered into at the beginning of the employment relationship. If the noncompete agreement is entered into after the employment relationship begins, it is not valid unless the employer furnished what is known as "independent consideration" to the employee. This usually consists of some additional compensation or other benefits to which the employee was not otherwise entitled.

If you have leverage when you're being hired, and you feel that the nondisclosure, nonsolicitation, or noncompete agreement is too restrictive, then try to negotiate the terms of those documents. If you are being hired by a major consulting company, unless you have a highly desirable skill-set, the company would be unlikely to change their standard agreement. However, if you're going to work for relatively small company, you have a much better chance of restricting the covenants in the noncompete agreement. There are times when the hiring manager wants the employee enough to change terminology that is otherwise too restrictive, so it can't hurt to ask. Again, if you have leverage, you have a greater chance of getting changes. If you have neither leverage nor a flexible hiring manager, you will have to live with the standard wording. However, if the company is known to be strict in its interpretation of noncompetes, and has pursued other individuals through the courts, then you would do well to press hard for changes. In such cases, even if you win in the court on the basis of enforceability, you may ultimately be the loser.

The most reasonable approach to a noncompete agreement is one that defines both specific time limitations and specific competitors. For example, an agreement might state that you can't work for the following three named competitors for a six-month period following termination. The combination of the time element and the list of restricted employers makes this a reasonable agreement. At the other end of the spectrum would be an agreement for an executive with twenty years' experience in the software industry stating that the executive could not work in that industry for one year. Since that is the area where the executive's career has been based, such an agreement would be too restrictive.

A principled executive will have no intention of disclosing secrets, and it's reasonable for the company to protect its employees, clients, and near-term prospects. However, it's not reasonable to prevent the executive from working in his or her area of expertise, so it's wise to offer a nonsolicitation agreement as an alternative to a noncompete as it truly protects the employer's interests.

If this is a sticking point with the company and they insist that you sign a noncompete agreement, you may want to take a step back and ask them to define their core concerns. What will the noncompete agreement provide them in terms of protection? If their desire is to prevent you from working in the industry for a certain period of time, this is unreasonable. On the other hand, if their desire is to prevent you from soliciting clients and recruiting employees, you can suggest that a nonsolicitation agreement directly addresses those concerns.

No one was ever happy that they signed a noncompete agreement; such agreements simply do not have the executive's interests at heart, and are intrinsically unfair.

◆ Preparation

While most executives think that salary, benefits, and equity are the most important areas on which to focus, noncompete agreements are as important as severance terms. If you have spent twenty years building your career and network in a specific industry, then get terminated and find yourself unable to pursue work in that industry for a long period of time, this could greatly inhibit your ability to secure a new job. If a potential new employer is aware of your noncompete restrictions, they will not want to take a chance on becoming involved in costly litigation to defend your position. Therefore, it is important to understand the various negotiating points within these agreements, and to use them as a framework for narrowing the potential restrictions. If you have already signed an overly restrictive noncompete agreement, remember that courts traditionally have looked unfavorably upon restrictions placed by companies on their executives' rights to find and make a living. However, courts will enforce noncompete agreements if:

- The company proves that it has a legitimate business interest to protect by restricting its executives' right to compete against it (i.e., preventing an employee from taking advantage of contacts or customer lists he or she has gained access to as a result of his or her employment);

- The restriction on the executive's right to compete is no greater than that necessary to protect the employer's business interest; and
- The covenant not to compete is supported by consideration, meaning that the employee received something in exchange for it.

Once you understand these key points, you will have a basis to negotiate the narrowest, fairest, and least restrictive terms within your nondisclosure, nonsolicitation, and noncompete agreements. Depending upon how formal or complex the document is, you may want to have a lawyer look at it.

◆ The Negotiation

When you go into any negotiation, be sure you know what you want to accomplish—the ideal solution—and negotiate from that basis. If you like the job but you don't want to sign a restrictive agreement, you need to tell the employer that up front and discuss your reasoning in advance. With many companies, not signing such an agreement is not an option: If you want the job, you must sign. In that case, you may be able to use the agreement as leverage for some other negotiating point. For example, before signing a noncompete agreement, you may press for a more extensive severance package, on the grounds that the noncompete would keep you from working within your chosen field in that area for a certain period of time.

Even if you can't negotiate to be exempted from the noncompete agreement, you should be able to negotiate for a very specific agreement. If the company's agreement includes blanket prohibitions, such as "salesperson for defense contractor," try to narrow it down: "salesperson for defense contractors A, B, or C" or "salesperson for defense contractor marketing products of types X, Y, or Z." If the agreement refers to the company's "clients," try to define "clients." Does this mean only someone with whom the company has a current business relationship, or does it include anyone with whom the company has discussed providing services? Again, the narrower the definition, the better.

Analysis

Analyze the situation, your interests, and those of the other party, and begin gathering information. You will need to develop answers to questions like these:

Key Questions

Self-Analysis

- Would I want to work in this industry/profession in the future?
- What would I do if I were legally restricted from working in this field?
- Can I support myself outside the industry for one or two years?
- What can I learn from past experience with noncompete agreeements?

Opportunity Analysis

- What are the time limits on the noncompete?
- What are the geographic limits on the noncompete?
- What type of work is limited by the noncompete?
- Who is included in the nonsolicitation agreement?

Planning

Use planning to establish your strategy, understand the other party's interests, and determine what options or alternatives would be acceptable outcomes. Ask yourself questions like these as part of your planning process:

Key Questions

- What kinds of information might the prospective employer not want me to share?
- Does the company make all employees sign noncompetes, or only employees at a certain level, or in certain areas?

Discussion

During the negotiation, these are some of the questions you should ask:

Questions to Ask

- Is the noncompete agreement negotiable? (This is often best phrased as a concern: "I have a concern with the length of time or geographic restriction, but I would be open to alternative definitions.")
- If employment terminates "not for cause," will you release me from the noncompete provisions?
- Can we narrow the time and geographic limits of the restraint?
- Can we limit the definition of the prohibited activity or prohibited employment?

◆ Outcome: Next Steps

Normally, nondisclosure, nonsolicitation, and noncompete agreements are introduced in the context of a written employment agreement or offer letter. These agreements are fairly standard; however, these are agreements that you must carefully review as they can have a considerable impact on your employability. You want to strike a balance between the company's interests and your own.

The nondisclosure/nonsolicitation/noncompete agreement shown in the excerpt that follows uses a common format. It defines the realm of confidential information and states that the executive may not disclose such information to any other party. An important clause to note is the New Developments/New Inventions clause. Typically, any invention or idea that you develop while employed by the company is deemed to be owned by the company even if you develop the invention or idea away from the company's office. If you have any prior inventions, it is important to tell the company about them before signing the agreement so that your prior inventions are specifically excluded from the provisions of this section.

The next section, Surrender of the Company's Materials Upon Separation, merely states that, upon separation, you will return all of the company's property, which includes marketing material, notes, drawings, manuals, etc.

The most important section to review and consider is the one titled Covenant Not to Compete. This section could have adverse long-term effects; it is strongly recommended that you have an attorney carefully review this section. An overly restrictive noncompete agreement may include a restriction on competition in any area in which the company does business; this is too broad and nonspecific. From an employee's perspective, it is better to enter into an agreement prohibiting the solicitation of the former employer's customers for a defined period of time. Under such an agreement, after you leave a company, you cannot call on any of your former employer's clients or accept any such client as a client of your new employer. It is important to have a clear definition of "client." Such a definition may include anyone with whom the company has actually signed an agreement to provide services, which is reasonable; however, some companies may also understand "client" to mean anyone with whom they have discussed providing services in the future, even if there is no current agreement. It's important to make sure that all the parameters are clear.

The next two sections, Solicitation of Company Employees After Separation and Solicitation of Company Customers/Clients, are common clauses that prevent you from recruiting other employees away from the company or soliciting the company's customers in the event of your departure or termination.

The overall goal of this section is to protect the company's intellectual property assets while not preventing the executive from making a living in the event that he or she leaves the company. It's important to understand what you're signing and the parameters of where you'll be restricted and where you have leeway. Future employers take noncompete agreements seriously; they will not want to become involved in expensive litigation with another company over any new employee.

Example as Excerpted from an Executive's Employment Agreement

6. Assignment of Invention, Nondisclosure, Nonsolicitation, and Noncompetition Agreement.

(a) Confidential Information and Materials. The Executive agrees that all information and materials acquired by him or her concerning the Company's business and the Company's customers are confidential and shall not be disclosed to any other person or used in any way that would be detrimental to the Company's business or to the business of the Company's customers. Such confidential information and materials include, without limitation, all information and materials belonging to, used by, or in the possession of the Company or its customers relating to: Company financial information, business strategies, pricing, customers, customer patient information and medical records, technology, programs, costs, employee compensation, marketing plans, developmental plans, computer programs, computer systems, inventions, and trade secrets of every kind and character.

(b) New Developments. The Executive agrees that during the course of his or her employment with the Company, he or she will promptly disclose to the Company all improvements, inventions, discoveries, innovations, systems, techniques, ideas, processes, programs, and other things which may be of assistance to the Company in its development of services or products, and which were made or conceived by the Executive alone or with others, while employed by the Company, regardless of whether developed on working time or personal time or whether developed at the Company's offices or the Executive's home (collectively referred to hereinafter as "New Developments"). The Executive agrees that all New Developments are the sole and exclusive property of the Company. The Executive agrees, upon the request of the Company, to do all lawful things reasonably necessary to ensure the Company's ownership of such New Developments including, without limitation, the execution of any necessary documents assigning and transferring to the Company and its assigns all of his or her rights, title, and interest in and to such New Developments.

c) Surrender of Company Material Upon Separation. The Executive agrees that upon separation of his or her employment with the Company, he or she will immediately surrender to the Company all property belonging to the Company. The Executive also agrees to surrender to the Company all personal notes, drawings, manuals, documents, photographs, or correspondence, including copies thereof, relating to any confidential information or New Developments which are in his or her possession or in the possession of an individual or entity under his or her control.

(d) Covenant Not to Compete.

A. While employed by the Company and for a period of twenty-four (24) months after the date of the Executive's separation from employment, the Executive shall not, within the United States, for himself or as an agent or employee of any business enterprise, directly or indirectly, be engaged in any activity or business which directly or indirectly competes with the business of the Company. The business of the Company is defined as ________________ throughout the United States.

B. The Executive represents and warrants to the Company that his or her experience and abilities are such that he or she can obtain employment in a business different from the business conducted by the Company. The Executive further represents and warrants that he or she understands that the restrictions contained in this Section ("Covenant Not to Compete") apply regardless of whether Executive's separation from the Company is voluntary or involuntary or is with cause or without cause.

C. This Covenant Not to Compete shall not prohibit the ownership by the Executive of stock of any publicly-held corporation (as hereinafter defined) so long as such stock comprises less than one percent (1%) of the issued and outstanding stock of the same class of the issuing corporation. For purposes of this Subsection, the term "publicly-held corporation" means a corporation which is subject to the periodic reporting requirements of Section 12(g) of the Securities Exchange Act of 1934, as amended.

D. The Executive acknowledges that the activities prohibited and the geographic and time restrictions imposed by the provisions of this Covenant Not to Compete are fair and reasonable and are reasonably required for the protection of the Company's legitimate business interests. In the event that any part of this Covenant Not to Compete is held to be unenforceable or invalid, the parties agree that a court of competent jurisdiction will designate geographic and/or time restrictions or proscribed activities as is deemed reasonable and will thereupon enforce the covenants as modified. It is the intent of the parties that the nature of the restrictions, the geographic scope of the restrictions, and the periods of time restrained be the maximum deemed to be fair and reasonable.

E. If, after separation of employment, the Executive violates this Covenant Not to Compete, the duration of this Covenant Not to Compete after separation of employment shall be computed from the date the Executive resumes compliance with this Covenant Not to Compete.

(e) Solicitation of Company Employees After Separation. The Executive agrees that, for a period of twenty-four (24) months after the separation of his or her employment with the Company, he or she will not, directly or indirectly (whether as a sole proprietor, partner, stockholder, director, officer, employee, or in any other capacity as principal or agent), do any of the following:

A. Hire, or attempt to hire for employment, in any business venture, any person who was an employee of the Company or any subsidiary or parent of the Company within the six (6) month period immediately preceding the Executive's separation of employment with the Company, or attempt to influence any such person to terminate such employment; or

B. In any other manner interfere with, disrupt, or attempt to disrupt the relationship, contractual or otherwise, between the Company or any subsidiary or parent of the Company and any of their employees.

(f) Solicitation of Company Customers/Clients. The Executive agrees that, for a period of twenty-four (24) months after the separation of his or her employment with the Company, he or she will not, directly or indirectly (whether as a sole proprietor, partner, stockholder, director, officer, employee, or in any other capacity as principal or agent) solicit the business of any of the Company's customers/clients. For the purposes of this Agreement, the Company's customers/clients shall be defined as any customer/client for which the Company has provided services during the twenty-four (24) month period immediately preceding the Executive's separation of employment with the Company or prepared a bid or proposal to provide services within the six (6) month period immediately preceding the Executive's separation of employment with the Company. Within thirty (30) days of the Executive's separation of employment, the Company shall provide the Executive with a list of the Company's Customers/Clients which fall within the prohibition of this provision.

Executive's Insight: Nondisclosure/ Nonsolicitation/Noncompete Agreement

Randy Grigg started his career in corporate banking, doing financing on leveraged buyouts, then moved to the corporate development area, working on mergers and acquisitions and joint ventures in Southeast Asia and Europe. He is now the managing director of a technology investment bank, specializing in merger and acquisitions advisory work with middle-market technology companies. The win–win principles exemplified in this excerpt are shown in the right-hand margin of the text.

"With my current company, we didn't discuss the noncompete agreement in advance; it was initially presented in the draft of the employment agreement. The initial discussion was about things like base salary and bonus; there's a myriad of other details that we didn't discuss, but that were covered in the document, so I wasn't surprised to find things in the document that we hadn't discussed.

"However, because the investment banking area was a new one for me, I didn't have a good grasp on whether or not this type of thing is standard in this industry. I had a good relationship with a few people in investment banking at other firms, so I called them and asked their opinion on what was or wasn't standard. Actually, what I heard from them was that it's unusual to have any sort of noncompete provisions in the investment banking world. I also spoke with a friend who is a lawyer; she said that you don't typically sign a noncompete agreement unless you also had a severance package in the event that you are terminated.

Principles in Action: Identify objective criteria.

"As I looked more closely at the noncompete agreement, I had some areas of concern. For one thing, the territory it covered was defined rather loosely as 'any area in which the company does business.' That kind of vague wording would be open to a dispute down the road. Another area of concern was the nonsolicitation of customers; it stated not only that I couldn't call any of their clients for twelve months following termination, but also that I couldn't accept any of their clients. The solicitation part is pretty standard, but usually, if you don't solicit a client—if the client comes to you and wants to work with you—then you don't have to turn them down. Also, the way they had defined 'client' was pretty broad; is a client someone with whom you've actually signed an agreement, or someone with whom you are working on an agreement, or just anyone with whom you have had any sort of discussion?

Principles in Action: Identify the fundamental problem.

"I wanted the terms of the agreement to be specific, but the agreement itself to be loose. I wanted the terms to be specific so that I know exactly what constitutes a breach, so I don't inadvertently breach the agreement. But I wanted the agreement itself to be as unrestrictive as possible. An example of an agreement that was both vague and restrictive would be one that says you are in breach if you have any interaction with a company with which the firm has had a relationship. That's vague in a number of ways; for example, what does 'a relationship' mean? Does that mean you've sent them a blind mailer? You've had a phone conversation with somebody there? You've signed them up to a contract? Because the wording is so vague, it can be interpreted very broadly, and thus would be very restrictive of your activities. An example of an agreement that was both specific and loose would be one that says you are in breach if you solicit business from a company that is, or has been, a client of the firm. This is specific: I know what is a breach, and what isn't. A breach involves a company that is actually signed up as a client, and a situation where I actually go out and solicit the client, not where they come to me without my solicitation.

Principles in Action: Identify your interests.

"After I read the proposed agreement, I had a friend who is a corporate attorney read the entire document and make comments on it, suggesting changes from my perspective. I sent the annotated agreement back to the company, and they reviewed it. We then went back and forth over it a few times on the phone, making changes and talking about other issues, until we finally got it resolved. My approach was not to be aggressive, but to try to get clarification; it's in nobody's interests to have a situation where we don't know what the document means. I also appealed to their sense of logic; given that the agreement didn't have a severance component, the noncompete couldn't be so restrictive that it kept me from getting a job for a significant period of time.

Principles in Action: Focus on interests, not positions.

Principles in Action: Understand the other party's interests.

"Of course, the noncompete was just one topic in a multi-faceted discussion. They took a very firm line on the noncompete agreement.

Essentially, their position was that, as a young firm, their relationships with other companies were their greatest asset, and they needed to be protected from someone walking away from the firm and using those relationships. In this area, they were much less flexible than in others. But there were trade-offs. Because they were unwilling to bend in terms of the noncompete, they were willing to give a little more in the area of overall compensation, bonus, and other benefits.

Principles in Action: Invent options for mutual gains.

"And while the noncompete agreement did remain in effect, it was also made more specific. For example, within thirty days following my termination, the company would be obligated to provide me with a list of clients so I would know exactly who fell into that category. The definition of what constitutes a referral source was made clearer. Some of the definitions were made a bit less restrictive, which was to my benefit. There were a lot of small changes. The bottom line is, although a noncompete agreement is not typical for this industry, there were other things in the overall package that were equally unusual and that balanced the equation for me.

"The key, in negotiating a noncompete agreement—or any other part of the employment agreement—is to focus on the big picture, not individual components; make sure that you get the best overall deal that you can. Focus on the relationship. Don't let the negotiation ruin the relationship coming in, because that's the most important thing. You can ask for a lot of things if you do it in the right way, if you're not threatening, or aggressive, or demanding—if you're asking for help in areas, and expressing legitimate concern. You can use your attorney's advice to your benefit here, say, 'I really don't know much about this area, but my attorney is telling me this is something I really shouldn't do.' Taking this approach deflects the issue to a third party. It suggests that it's not really you who is raising the issue, it's somebody else, which takes the personal element out of the discussion. And always, always end the discussions on a friendly note, something light, so neither party leaves the

Principles in Action: Focus on the end goal.

Principles in Action: Separate the people from the problem.

room or gets off the phone thinking only about the dispute you are having.

"In this type of negotiation, preparation is critical. You have to know your position and your arguments very well, and to have a good basis for them. You have to understand what you're willing to take at the end of the day—what's your walkaway point—so you know how to respond to their responses. I did have other options at the time, in case the negotiation didn't work out. One was as a partner in a venture capital firm, and the other was in investment banking. However, both of these options were in other cities, and I definitely wanted to get back to this city. The people I was negotiating with knew that, and I'm sure they used it to their advantage. But they also knew, in broad terms, that I had alternatives, so that tempered their ability to use my desire to relocate here. And finally, your communication style and approach have to focus on the positive. If you keep the long-term relationship in mind, you'll both end up happy with the agreement."

Principles in Action: Identify your alternatives.

Chapter Summary: Nondisclosure/Nonsolicitation/ Noncompete Agreement

- **Nondisclosure agreements.** These agreements help to ensure that an employee or former employee won't divulge trade secrets, formulas, client lists, process secrets, business approaches, or product knowledge that could benefit the employer's competition.
- **Nonsolicitation agreements.** These agreements protect the employer's interest by preventing a former employee from soliciting business from company clients or from recruiting employees.
- **Noncompete agreements.** A noncompete agreement is most often used to keep former employees from working for a competitor for a predefined period of time.
- **Understand the parameters of your noncompete.** Look at time limits, geographical restrictions, and what type of

work is being restricted as you evaluate the reasonableness of the document.

- **Clearly define the prohibited business activity.** Attempt to limit your restrictions to the minimum extent (both in terms of time and geography) necessary to protect the employer's legitimate business interest. If the company's agreement includes blanket prohibitions, try to narrow them down.
- **If possible, use a nonsolicitation agreement rather than a noncompete agreement.** Understand the company's core concerns for requesting a noncompete, and offer a nonsolicitation as an alternative, since it truly protects the employer's interests.
- **Review your noncompete and/or nonsolicitation agreement with an attorney.** These agreements can adversely affect your career for years to come if not reviewed carefully, so it is strongly recommended that you have your attorney's input.

CHAPTER TEN

Severance Package

I make my case for a severance package at the beginning.
—Martha Powers,
Partner

◆ The Challenge and Overview

What happens if you join a company as the vice president of marketing, and six months later there is a significant change in ownership and management, which results in material changes to your position? This is the type of situation that makes it critical to negotiate a severance package in advance. Severance packages are not just designed to protect you in case you are terminated; they also protect you in the event that your job changes due to circumstances you can't control.

Severance refers to the continuation of wages and benefits for a specified period of time (the severance period) after the termination of employment, whether the departure is voluntary or involuntary. Severance may include a combination of wage/salary continuation and continuation of health insurance and other benefits at the employer's expense. While you don't want to enter into a new employment relationship thinking about possible termination, it's important to discuss and negotiate your severance package prior to joining the company. It's important for two reasons: 1) You have the greatest leverage before you are hired; and

2) Your employment could be vulnerable, either because of the changing needs of the company or due to the unpredictable economy.

Without a written agreement, severance is usually provided at the discretion of the employer. Often, severance is only provided if the employee agrees to release the company from any claim that the employee may have against the employer related to the employment relationship. As an at-will employee, if you do not address your severance prior to joining the company, you will have very limited rights to severance in most jurisdictions.

> ***Example:*** Jordan Baker accepted a position as senior vice president for BleedingEdge Software, a medium-sized technology company. Before joining the company, he negotiated a competitive salary, excellent benefits, and a generous stock options package. The company performed well during his first eight months with them; however, due to external economic factors, BleedingEdge's third round of funding did not come through. The board of directors imposed an immediate 30 percent reduction of staff, and the most recently hired senior management staff were among the first to be laid off. Although Jordan's performance had been stellar, he was among those let go. Jordan had not asked for a severance package when he was hired. The company offered two weeks severance and one month continuation of his company-paid health benefits. In addition, Jordan had to forfeit his entire stock options package, since he had not been with the company long enough for any vesting. Jordan tried to negotiate a longer severance package once he received his notice, but at that stage, he had little leverage. After several back-and-forth discussions, the company agreed to provide Jordan an additional two weeks' severance. This meant Jordan, a senior manager, now had a total of one month's financial support while he looked for a commensurate position.

Thinking about your severance package is not usually a pleasant prospect; some people equate it to planning your own funeral. However, this is not the right way to perceive this area of your employment agreement. One thing to keep in mind is that the severance clause is not invoked only if you are fired for reasons other than cause; it can also be activated if the company is acquired. In such a case, this clause could be your "golden parachute."

> ***Example:*** Big Biotech acquired Great Idea, a small biotech company, because of Great Idea's intellectual property assets. As part of their consolidation, Big Biotech decided to replace Alex Farrell, the CEO of Great Idea. However, Alex still had two years remaining on her employment contract. She had negotiated a severance package that entitled her to full vesting on her stock options and eighteen months of full salary, health benefits, and car allowance. Alex had anticipated all possible scenarios in her contract. Although she was disappointed to leave the company she had helped build, she was not left without significant remuneration.

◆ Preparation

Before you engage in your severance discussion, it's prudent to determine what is important to you with respect to the overall terms and conditions of your severance package. Plan for enough time, in the event that you are terminated, to find a new job at your current or higher level. Consider your monthly expenses; be sure you understand what will happen with your stock options; determine whether you are receiving any benefits as an employee that you would need to have continued if you are terminated. Calculate your living expenses on paper; make a list of other key issues you need to resolve if this clause is exercised due to change in management or because you are terminated.

◆ The Negotiation

To negotiate this area, you should first build a framework so that you'll feel at ease when discussing this sometimes uncomfortable topic. If you've already thought about these issues, you'll be more natural and articulate when explaining your points to the employer.

Analysis

Analyze the situation, your interests, and those of the other party, and begin gathering information. You will need to develop answers to questions like these:

Key Questions

Self-Analysis

- If I am terminated for reasons other than cause, how long will it take me to get another job in my area of expertise?
- What are my family's monthly living expenses?
- Do I have sufficient savings to meet my obligations during the job search period?
- What will I need in order to find a new job?

Opportunity Analysis

- Am I an at-will employee who can be terminated at any time for any reason, or am I subject to an employment contract with specific provisions for termination?
- Have any changes in control (due to merger, acquisition, or sale of the company) been discussed during interviews?
- What is the employer's past experience with terminating staff at my level?
- How has the employer handled staff reductions during downsizing, reorganizations, or mergers/acquisitions?

Planning

Use planning to establish your strategy, understand the other party's interests, and determine what options or alternatives would be acceptable outcomes. Ask yourself questions like these as part of your planning process:

Questions to Ask

- Is there a standard severance package (based on number of years of service) or are severance packages custom-designed?
- What options are available as part of a severance package? Continued salary, benefits, outplacement, coaching, access to company or other office facilities, etc.?

Discussion

During the negotiation, these are some of the questions you should ask:

Key Questions

- Does the company provide outplacement services?
- Could the company provide benefits in lieu of severance?
- Can you describe your severance package (length, benefits, etc.)?
- Is severance only paid when terminated "not for cause"?
- What is the definition of cause? Be as specific as possible.
- Is there a difference in the severance if there is a change in control of the company?
- Is severance through normal payroll or in a lump sum?
- Does the company continue to provide fringe benefits during the severance period?

◆ Outcome: Next Steps

When people take a new job, they usually do not like to anticipate that things might go wrong; this can lead to a failure to negotiate effectively on termination provisions and severance packages. This component of the agreement is extremely important. The excerpt that follows is a solid structure that can be used as a basis for negotiation.

The first section describes the terminating events, such as expiration of the employment agreement, or for cause events, which may involve felonious acts committed by the executive or conduct bringing the company into public disgrace. One important clause is the "opportunity to cure" clause; this gives the executive the opportunity to fix any problems that the company perceives. The cure period should be explicitly stated, ranging from ten to twenty business days. Obviously, it is more favorable from the executive's perspective to have the longest cure period possible.

"Effect of Termination" (Section 5) details the process that occurs once a terminating event has been triggered. If an executive is terminated "for cause" as defined in Section 4.2, then he or she will not be eligible for the severance package, since he or she was the reason for the termination, either due to a fraudulent act or due to poor performance that was clearly defined but not cured within the stated cure period.

"Termination by Company Other than for Cause" is an important clause. This is where the benefits and severance payout to the executive are defined. If the executive is terminated without "cause," then the company must pay the executive the severance package compensation and benefits for a predefined period of time; this can range from as little as three to as much as eighteen months. This area is completely negotiable; obviously, the executive should negotiate for the longest period of time due to the many factors involved in finding another executive-level job. Another key point is that if the executive is terminated for no fault of his or her own, then the company must take care of the executive for an extended period of time to compensate for high cost of living expenses.

A secondary component of the not for cause section involves stock options. This can vary from one employment agreement to the next because each company's incentive stock option (ISO) agreement varies. Typically, the employee will have the opportunity to exercise his or her vested options within ninety days of termination and the unvested portion will be forfeited; however, the specifics will be defined in the ISO agreement. This can be a negotiating point where the executive says that if he or she is terminated for no fault of his or her own, then he or she should be fully vested and have the option to exercise all options within a certain window of time. There have been extreme circumstances where an executive is about to become vested in a significant portion of his or her options, but the company terminates the executive just before the vesting period and some of the options must be forfeited. It is extremely important to understand these clauses before accepting employment. If the company will not negotiate on this point, this should give you pause as to their underlying reasons for standing by this clause. It is strongly recommended that you ask your attorney about these issues.

Example as Excerpted from an Executive's Employment Agreement

4. Employment Termination. The employment of the Executive by the Company pursuant to this Agreement shall terminate upon the occurrence of any of the following:

4.1 Expiration of the Employment Period in accordance with Section 1;

4.2 At the election of the Company, for Cause (as defined below), immediately upon written notice by the Company to the Executive. For the purposes of this Section 4.2, "Cause" means (i) the commission by Executive of a felony or a crime involving moral turpitude or the intentional commission of any other act or omission involving dishonesty or fraud with respect to the Company or any of their customers or suppliers, (ii) conduct by Executive tending to bring the Company into substantial public disgrace or disrepute not cured within ten (10) business days after written notice thereof, (iii) substantial and repeated failure by Executive to perform duties of the office held by Executive as reasonably directed by the Board not cured within ten (10) business days after written notice thereof, (iv) substantial and repeated poor performance by Executive of his duties as specified in written notice from the Board specifying such deficiencies and the required actions needed to cure such poor performance, and not cured within ten (10) business days after written notice thereof, or (v) any material breach of this Agreement or the agreements attached hereto as Exhibits A, B, and C, not cured within ten (10) business days after written notice thereof from the Company. The cure periods specified in this Section 4 shall not apply to any breach which by its nature is not susceptible to a cure.

4.3 Upon the death or thirty (30) days following the disability of the Executive. As used in this Agreement, the term "disability" shall mean the inability of the Executive, due to a physical or mental disability, for a period of ninety (90) substantially consecutive days, to perform the essential functions of his position as Company President and Chief Executive Officer. A determination of disability shall be made by a physician satisfactory to both the Executive and the Company, provided that if the Executive and the Company do not agree on a physician, the Executive and the Company shall each select a physician and these two together shall select a third physician, whose determination as to disability shall be binding on all parties;

4.4 At the election of the Executive, upon not less than sixty (60) days prior written notice of termination other than for a material breach of this Agreement by the Company; or

4.5 At the election of the Executive for a material breach of this Agreement by the Company, which such breach has not been cured within ten (10) business days after written notice thereof from the Executive.

5. <u>Effect of Termination</u>.

5.1 <u>Termination for Cause or at Election of Executive</u>. In the event the Executive's employment is terminated by the Company pursuant to Section 4.2 or by the Executive pursuant to Section 4.4, the Company shall pay to the Executive the compensation and benefits otherwise payable to him under Section 3 through the last day of his actual employment by the Company.

5.2 Termination for Death or Disability. If the Executive's employment is terminated by death or because of disability pursuant to Section 4.3, the Company shall pay to the estate of the Executive or to the Executive, as the case may be, the compensation which would otherwise be payable to the Executive up to the end of the month in which the termination of his employment because of death or disability occurs.

5.3 Termination by Company Other than for Cause.

(a) If the Executive's employment is terminated by the Company other than for Cause as defined in Section 4.2, the Company shall pay to the Executive the compensation and benefits otherwise payable to him under Section 3 through the last day of his actual employment by the Company, and shall continue to pay his Base Salary at the rate then in effect for a period of eight (8) months as severance pay.

(b) The Executive's rights with respect to the Executive's stock options in the event of termination shall be governed by the terms of the Incentive Stock Option Grant Agreement applicable thereto.

Executive's Insight: Severance

Martha Powers is a partner in a Web development firm. Previously, she was a principal and partner at leading management consulting firms. The win–win principles exemplified in this excerpt are shown in the right-hand margin of the text.

Principles in Action: Know the company.

"The company I am with had gone through a massive restructuring in the year before I joined, and had just brought in a turnaround team three months before I joined. I was aware of this, and of all the changes in this industry. Because of this, I raised the issue of severance during the salary negotiation. My concerns were what would happen in the case of a change in either ownership or management.

"When I raised the issue, I placed it firmly in the context of the stability of the company. They had gone through massive changes. I was moving from a stable, reliable company, where I was receiving a substantial income, to a much more high-risk situation.

"The company had absolutely no problem with the question of severance. It's really standard at an executive level. The thing is, if you don't bring it up, it's not offered to you, but if you do, they understand.

"The concerns I voiced were that, at my level as an executive, and in terms of my salary level in the marketplace, if the company was restructured or sold and my position changed, it would take me at least three to six months to find a new position. The company agreed to give me six months severance.

Principles in Action: Identify your interests.

"In terms of preparation, the biggest thing was to be informed. I generally read about four newspapers a day, so I'm pretty well aware of what's going on with jobs and cuts and so forth. I'm also fairly up-to-date with knowing what other people are negotiating right now, and what not to forget, especially in a high-risk environment.

"I think the biggest thing is to be aware of expectations. What are their expectations for me in the job, what is the role? I get that clearly defined up front. I've been in situations before where there was a kind of 'bait and switch' situation—you're told that if you come in at this, you'll be promoted in three months, but then the promotion doesn't happen. I make sure to clearly define my role and my responsibilities. Also, I do my due diligence in terms of talking to people who have left the company, talking to people within the company, and looking at the industry in general to see what is going on in terms of severance packages, stock option vesting clauses, and so forth.

Principles in Action: Identify the company's interests.

Principles in Action: Research the company.

"And then, of course, I always have my personal lawyer review my contracts. That's always a key step, to ask, 'Am I forgetting anything? What else are you seeing out there in terms of employment contracts?'

"Some people find the topic of a severance package unpleasant. My take on it is influenced by my experience. I graduated from business school in May 1987, and moved into a strong market. Then came the October 'market correction.' Within a year, all the people who had graduated with me were on their second jobs. We had worked hard, but many companies handled the whole thing badly. If they had treated employees with dignity, they might have kept some employee loyalty going into the '90s, but that didn't happen. I've always kept that unpleasantness in the back of my mind; you never know what can happen.

Principles in Action: Identify the core problems.

"Still, for a lot of people, raising the issue of severance is difficult. You're in a constructive and positive environment, getting excited about taking the job. People wonder if they should bring it up. It's a bit like asking for a prenuptial agreement before a wedding—making plans for things to go sour.

"I always do my own little presentation to myself as if I were on the other side of the table. I prepare key bullet points, such as, 'Your company has gone through downsizing three times, this is a high-risk situation, this is typically what's going on in the industry right now, and I would hope that we could put this into any negotiations that we do.' I come to the negotiation very prepared.

Principles in Action: Be prepared for negotiations.

"In negotiations in general, I like to be informed, prepared, and collaborative. I'm not confrontational at all, but I do my due diligence, go in with my expectations clear, and make my case at the beginning. I negotiate everything up front, and then make sure it's all documented. And then I always have an employment attorney look at it, just so I'm not missing things.

"Basically, do your homework, understand what you want when you go in, and don't be afraid. Especially at certain times in the economy, it's OK to do it and ask for forgiveness later. You have to keep the emotions out of the negotiation. I've seen people at my level come in but feel

Principles in Action: Maintain your composure.

uncomfortable asking for severance. When they find out that I've done it, they're surprised. My response is, 'I did my homework.' Especially when there is a previous working relationship, people fear that asking for a severance package is like saying, 'I don't trust you.' In tough times, just going on trust doesn't work. You see too many things like downsizing and layoffs, and some people get hurt. So asking for a severance package isn't a question of trust, it's just being realistic. You just have to say, 'Look, you never know what's going to happen. I'm really excited about the position, but there are no guarantees. I'm just looking out for myself because I want to be able to work with my whole focus on the job, without having to worry about things like downsizing.' "

Chapter Summary: Severance

- **What is severance?** Severance refers to the continuation of wages and benefits for a specified period of time after the termination of employment, whether the departure is voluntary or involuntary. Severance may include a combination of continuation of wages/salary, health insurance, and other benefits at the employer's expense.
- **Why severance?** Severance protects you if there is a significant change in ownership and management and your position materially changes.
- **If you don't ask, you don't get.** If you do not discuss your severance package while negotiating the terms of your employment agreement, it probably won't be offered; however, if you ask for a severance package, you'll most likely find it one of the easier and more standard negotiations at an executive level.
- **Do your research.** See what others are receiving in the industry; typical severance packages range from three to six months.
- **Negotiate your severance package in advance.** Use the change in control concern as a way to raise the uncomfortable topic of severance before joining the company.

CHAPTER ELEVEN

The Employment Agreement

The employment agreement is a way to make sure you're protected, primarily because you are giving up other opportunities to take this one.

—Steve Peck, CFO

◆ The Challenge and Overview

Employment contracts are legal documents, designed to protect both the employer and the employee. These documents go well beyond post-employment restrictions. Employment contracts are usually used when someone is being hired for an executive-level position. They govern the employment relationship and outline what is expected of both the employee and the employer.

Employment contracts will define a number of issues, such as compensation in all of its forms, job responsibilities, expectations of the employer, and the employee's severance package. There is always a predefined time period during which the employment contract will be in effect. Often, an employment contract will also outline special arrangements made between the employee and employer. There's a comfort in having an employment contract, because the work relationship is well defined and laid out.

Whenever you're asked to sign a legal document, it's vital that you have a good understanding of what the document entails. If you don't understand a document, you should seek the advice of an attorney. Never sign anything that you don't understand or that you haven't read; you could be agreeing to a legal obligation that you'll be required to uphold. If the document is created by the employer (or the employer's legal advisers), it will certainly protect the employer; it is up to you to ensure that it also protects you, as the employee.

Your negotiating position is at its strongest after you have been offered a job, but before you have accepted the terms of the offer. Use this window of opportunity to set the parameters for your future with the company.

Terms of Employment Agreements

Arbitration Clauses

Many employment contracts and other legal documents related to employment issues contain *arbitration clauses,* which are designed to reduce legal costs and to prevent frivolous lawsuits. These clauses state that in the event of a disagreement between the two parties, instead of going to court, an arbitrator will be used to settle a claim. In some cases, arbitration is legally binding; in others, arbitration that doesn't settle a matter can be appealed in a traditional courtroom.

Arbitration clauses favor companies. Their purpose is the quick, economical, and confidential resolution of a dispute between the executive and the company. If you are terminated and feel you were treated unfairly, as an employee, you want a chance of a court verdict or a big settlement. These settlements can range from $5,000 to $25,000+, because it will cost the company the same amount to litigate. Most importantly, the company seeks to avoid any public humiliation or internal strife. So, as an employee, you'd rather not see an arbitration clause. If the employer asks for it, you generally cannot say "no," but it's valuable to understand its significance. Most employment attorneys who represent employees will not be happy to see such clauses because they limit the exposure of the company and decrease the executive's leverage in the event that there is a dispute after termination.

Before signing any legal document with an arbitration clause, make sure you understand what it means. Likewise, any legal wording that discusses how disagreements or legal issues will be dealt with should be examined carefully. Be careful about agreeing to a city or state where litigation will take place, or agreeing to cover the legal expenses of the other party if you lose the court case.

Employment Status

Employment agreements typically specify whether an individual is an "at-will" employee or whether the individual is employed for a specific period of time. In an at-will employment relationship, the relationship is at the "will" of the parties; either party may terminate the relationship for any reason or no reason, at any time, with or without notice. An at-will employee has no guarantee of continued employment or employment for a specific period of time. Employment at will is the opposite of employment for a specific period of time. Under an at-will employment relationship, the employer may terminate the employee at any time with or without reason so long as the reason for the termination is not prohibited by law (e.g., an employer may terminate an employee because of the color of the employee's shirt, but not because of the color of the employee's skin).

The at-will employment relationship is lost when there is an agreement requiring "cause" prior to termination of the employment relationship. Cause is frequently defined as including, among other things, job abandonment, conviction for a crime of dishonesty or moral turpitude, insubordination, conduct negatively affecting the goodwill or business reputation of the employer, and failure to give a high level of service to the employer's customers. "Not for cause" refers to termination at the discretion of the employer without attributing reasons for the decision. It is very common in at-will employment relationships to terminate an employee without cause. It may be to the employee's advantage to have a vague definition of cause as it may be more difficult for an employer to determine when it has cause to terminate an employee.

These days most employees, even executives, are at-will employees because this reduces the long-term liability for the company in the event of downsizing or if the company wishes to terminate an employee for performance reasons.

Nondisclosure, Nonsolicitation, Noncompete, Termination, and Severance

The employment agreement will also contain provisions regarding nondisclosure, nonsolicitation, noncompetition, dispute resolution, whether "cause" is required for termination, and severance, if appropriate. Nondisclosure agreements help to ensure that an employee or former employee won't divulge trade secrets, formulas, client lists, process secrets, business approaches, or product knowledge that could benefit the employer's competition. A noncompete agreement is most often used to keep an employee from competing with a former employer following the termination of the employment relationship. A nonsolicitation agreement ensures that a former employee does not solicit business from the former employer's clients, or try to recruit employees from within the company, for a set period of time.

It has become common practice for employers to require new employees to sign noncompete, nondisclosure, and/or nonsolicitation agreements upon being hired. They are somewhat standard in many industries and usually protect the employer after an employee leaves his or her job. When signing any type of legal document related to employment, make sure that the document is reasonable in terms of what it restricts. If you are about to sign a noncompete agreement, the period of time you are restricted from working in a similar job at a competing company must be reasonable for it to be enforced by the courts. Look at time limits, geographical restrictions, and what type of work is being restricted as you evaluate the reasonableness of the document. The term "reasonable" should be clearly defined in the document.

Standard employment agreements often don't include a severance clause. However, it is very much to your advantage to have such a clause included, to make sure that your needs will be met in the event that the company is acquired and your position materially changes, or you are terminated for some other reason.

Always take time to understand and, if appropriate, negotiate the terms of this area of your employment agreement. It is very important to get all details of employment specified in the employment agreement; in the event of a dispute, this agreement will be the document referenced. This is discussed in much greater detail in the relevant chapters.

◆ Preparation

If you are aiming for an executive-level position, you should negotiate for an employment agreement/contract. As an executive, you will probably be working long hours and making certain sacrifices for the company in order to increase its value. To be able to do this, you need to have a certain sense of security. However, you need to balance security and flexibility. If security is most important to you, negotiate for the longest term of employment possible, ranging from two years to five years. Depending upon the position, the size of the company, and company philosophy, this may or may not be an accepted practice. Try to find out about the company's policies, either through your recruiter or by asking about company philosophies. If you engage the interviewer in talking about the company's needs, you can get a sense of the importance of the tasks at hand.

Other important points to consider before going into your employment agreement discussions are covered in preceding chapters. They include salary, stock options, bonuses, benefits, relocation expenses, nondisclosure/nonsolicitation/noncompete agreements, and severance packages. If you think through these issues in advance, you will be much more at ease while negotiating.

Remember, this is a collaborative negotiation, not an adversarial one; you will ultimately have to work for the company, so it's important that both parties leave the table feeling satisfied. Otherwise, feelings of frustration can arise that do not go away, but grow deeper, posing problems down the line.

◆ The Negotiation

Your formal employment agreement negotiations begin as soon as there is any discussion about salary needs and job responsibility, so be aware of what you say and how you say it early on in the process. If you see signs of concrete interest on the employer's behalf, be sure you thoroughly understand your needs in terms of compensation, benefits, and so forth. You should also be sure you understand what the employer seeks in terms of objectives for the person who will fill the new role. This demonstrates that you have listened to their needs. Then, as you negotiate different areas of your employment agreement, you can raise points that focus on mutual interests, not positions. Although you may disagree about certain salary or benefit requirements, you both have the same interests in mind: to work together and to contribute to the success of the company.

It is essential that you think about all the issues that are important to you up front, rather than coming back repeatedly to negotiate more points. This guide provides a framework for all the key areas of your package. Choose the ones that are most important to you, and make sure they are included in the employment agreement.

◆ Analysis

Analyze the situation, your interests, and those of the other party, and begin gathering information. Consider your own interests, and those of the other party, by doing a self-analysis and an opportunity analysis. You will need to develop answers to questions like these:

Key Questions

Self-Analysis

- Do I prefer an extended employment contract that offers greater long-term security or a shorter commitment that offers greater flexibility?
- Which elements of the employment agreement are my highest priorities? What do I want? What do I need?

Opportunity Analysis

- What terms of employment have been discussed in interviews (title, responsibilities, salary, standard benefits, etc.)?
- How much variety is there in the benefits being offered?

Planning

Use planning to establish your strategy, understand the other party's interests, and determine what options or alternatives would be acceptable outcomes. Ask yourself questions like these as part of your planning process:

Key Questions

- What do I want?
- What terms of employment would I truly value? (time versus money, professional development versus perks?)
- What is my BATNA? How do other opportunities compare to what's being offered?
- Has the employer standardized all of the company's employment offers, or is there room for negotiation and customization?

Discussion

During the negotiation, you can get new information in two ways: through questions you ask the interviewer, and through unsolicited information the interviewer shares as part of the discussion. These are some of the questions you should ask and information you should listen for:

Questions to Ask

- Can you frame the key terms of the employment agreement?
- What provisions exist if the position materially changes due to a company restructuring or a merger or acquisition?
- [If relocating] What is your relocation policy?
- What is your stock options policy?
- What is the core benefits package (health, life, 401(k), vacation)?
- To whom does the position report?
- What happened to the person who was formerly in the position? (Listen for references to termination and how the employer refers to past employees, as this can reveal the individual's level of respect for employees and their relationship to the employer.)
- If the last person didn't work out, what happened to the person before him or her? If things didn't work out

repeatedly, is the problem that the company is unclear about what it was looking for?

- Does the company conduct performance reviews?
- How often are reviews performed—every three months? Six months? Annually?
- Are performance reviews done at the same time for everyone or on the anniversary date of employment? (If all reviews are done at the same time there's a greater chance of your review actually being on time; too often they fall through the cracks and end up being months late.)
- Who performs the review (direct supervisor, department head, CEO, etc.)?

Information to Listen For

You should understand and get clarification on all of the following areas if there is any ambiguity:

- Title and key responsibilities
- Salary
- Bonus
- At-will employment status versus contractual term of employment

◆ Outcome: Next Steps

There are many components to successfully negotiating your employment agreement. The most fundamental are the length of the agreement and the title/capacity in which you will serve. The term of employment is important because it provides you with security and a level of commitment from the company. Also, in the event of an acquisition, it gives you leverage and negotiating power if the acquirer wishes to replace the management team. If you have a year and a half remaining on your contract, at a $150,000 salary, a clear employment agreement would mean that the acquirer would have to pay your maximum of $225,000, or buy out your contract for a mutually acceptable amount. You should also make sure that you refer to the stock options section in the event that there is a change in control; you want to ensure that any unvested stock options become vested if the company is sold.

It might seem that title/capacity is so basic that it doesn't bear mentioning. However, it is important to clearly define your role and duties. Again, if the company is acquired, your role might change materially. In that case, you can exercise your "termination for non-cause" clause. If you neglect to pay attention to this, you may be tied to a two- or three-year commitment in a position that does not reflect what you were originally hired to do. Therefore, it is critical that you state what role you will perform and that any other role that is materially different will not bind you to the terms of the agreement and will not cause you to be in breach of the agreement if you choose to leave.

Example as Excerpted from an Executive's Employment Agreement

1. Term of Employment. The Company hereby agrees to employ the Executive, and the Executive hereby accepts employment with the Company, upon the terms set forth in this Agreement, for the period commencing May ___, 2001 (the "Commencement Date") and ending on April 31, 2004 (the "Termination Date"), unless sooner terminated in accordance with the provisions of Section 4 (such period, as it may be extended, being referred to as the "Employment Period"). Upon expiration of the initial term, the Employment Period shall automatically extend for additional one-year terms, unless the Executive or the Company gives ninety (90) days' advance written notice to the other of its election not to extend the term.

2. Title; Capacity. The Executive shall serve and be employed as President and Chief Executive Officer of the Company and shall be based in the District of Columbia office. In his capacity as Chief Executive Officer of the Company, the Executive shall report directly to the Company's Board of Directors (the "Board") and shall have primary authority and responsibility, subject to the control of the Board, for operational control, strategic planning and implementation, and marketing for the Company. As President, the Executive shall initially serve

as a nonvoting member of the Board until the next regularly scheduled election of directors, where he will stand for election as a full voting member of the Board.

Executive's Insight: Employment Agreement

Steve Peck has been CFO for both private and public companies. He is currently managing director and CEO of a venture fund. Here, he talks about his experience negotiating employment agreements. The win–win principles exemplified in this excerpt are shown in the right-hand margin of the text.

"The employment agreement is a way to make sure you're protected, primarily because you are giving up other opportunities to take this one. You want to make sure that the commitment is not just an emotional one, but one that is legally binding. The employment agreement both protects you and makes sure both parties are clear on the terms of your employment, the various benefits, the severance agreement, and so forth.

Principles in Action: Identify your interests.

"With my current position, I requested an employment agreement up front, and there was no argument about it at all. Both my attorney and my partner's attorney worked together to resolve the wording of the agreement.

"For me, the most important part of the agreement is the description of the responsibilities. In most cases, you want to be perfectly clear as to what you are expected to accomplish. That's critical, so that both parties understand your direction. After that, you need to look at income level, salary, bonus, and other benefits, including stock options and ownership in the company. And you need to be aware at the outset that things don't always work out, so you need to address the severance package.

"In preparing for a discussion, you have to first determine your personal needs: What are you looking for? Your needs will be different at different stages of your career. At this point, I'm looking for some fairly large hits and not so much

Principles in Action: Identify your needs.

long-term play. Fifteen years ago, I was looking more for an ongoing perspective.

"You always want to go into negotiations knowing you have other options. One thing you learn in business is, there's never a deal until it's done. Even though both sides are very, very serious about wanting to make that deal, you never really know what sort of snag may come into play that will absolutely kill the deal. So you never want to have just one deal on the table. Also, having other options gives you a level of confidence to push harder for all the points you want; if you can't get them, you have the choice of either backing off from those points or simply saying 'The deal isn't going to work,' and moving on to these other deals.

Principles in Action: Identify your BATNA.

Principles in Action: Be ready to walk away.

"In my most recent employment agreement, there were two hurdles. One was the level of return that my partner requested initially. I didn't feel that the return he wanted was possible in the time frame he wanted—two years. I felt the return rate was so onerous that I couldn't possibly live with it. Basically, I said that those returns weren't possible within two years on a start-up business—five years, maybe, but not two. So if he thought he could get that rate in two years from somebody else, that would be great, but I wasn't the person who could deliver it. My objection was twofold. First, agreeing to that rate would be setting myself up for failure. And second, because we are a venture group, I always felt we needed at least three to five years to prove ourselves. Eventually, we agreed to a two-year deal at a different return rate. This added more burden on me, but at the same time it gave me the benefit of getting into the venture community and meeting all the players.

Principles in Action: Focus on interests, not positions.

Principles in Action: Invent options for mutual gain.

"The second hurdle was my salary, which was more than he normally paid. However, the amount he was offering was just not something I could work with. He suggested a compromise: For the first year, my nominal salary was the amount he

Principles in Action: Identify your needs.

had offered, but he gave me an advance to cover the difference. Then, in the second year, my salary would be the amount I had wanted for the first year.

"In general terms, when you look at an employment agreement, you need to understand what you personally need. From a salary perspective, what do you need in order to live on a day-to-day basis? What do you think is a fair compensation for various successes and as rewards for reaching milestones? When dealing with a sole proprietor type organization, if the assets of the organization are not particularly strong, get the personal guarantee of the entrepreneur with whom you are signing the agreement.

"The severance package is an essential part of the employment agreement. How long a package you get depends on what level you're at; at my level, anything less than a year would be unacceptable. If you're a director, maybe a vice president, then a six-month severance would be worthwhile. Noncompete clauses are also important, especially from the employer's point of view. You need to be willing to sign a noncompete. At several companies, I've had a two-year noncompete, because in my position I have access to a lot of valuable information that could hurt the organization.

Principles in Action: Identify the company's interests.

"During the actual discussion process, it's important to understand where the employer is coming from, what the culture at the company is; you don't want to be asking for things that are totally at odds with the company's culture. There are a couple of ways to do this. With the Internet, you can get so much information about most companies, so while you're doing your basic research on the company to understand their operation, you should also look at the backgrounds of the officers of the organization—their education, their business background. This will start to give you a sense of the individuals that you are dealing with. Looking at the types of businesses that the company is associated with tells you something about the company, as well. But part of it comes from your interviewing them, not just the other way around. You need to determine whether you want to be with them. You need to do your due diligence with the company. Don't just talk to the person who is going to make the

Principles in Action: Research the company.

final decision, talk to other players within the team, as well. Ask who their vendors are, who they do business with. At a certain level, vice president or higher, you might even ask if you can call some of their vendors and talk with them about the relationship. Ask the right questions to find out, 'Am I really a good fit for this company?'

"Once you have made sure that your personal needs are being met in the employment agreement, have your attorney review it."

Chapter Summary: Employment Agreement

- **What are employment agreements?** Employment agreements are designed to protect both the employer and the employee. They should include specifics on compensation, job responsibilities, severance, bonuses, benefits, and relocation.
- **Identify the areas that are most important in advance.** Prioritize what you need to have as opposed to what would be nice to have.
- **Focus on defining your title, role, and responsibilities.** In the event of an acquisition, you want to ensure that your role will not materially change; if it does, you want the ability to exercise your exit or severance clause.
- **Carefully consider the length of commitment.** Depending upon your career goals, you should determine if you want a short- or long-term agreement because, once you sign it, you are committed.
- **Seek legal advice before signing your agreement.** You're making a long-term investment, so be sure you fully understand all the parameters of the agreement.

CHAPTER TWELVE

Annual Reviews

I want to be in there advocating for my career, not just letting it happen to me.
—Jeffrey Clegg,
Senior Manager

◆ The Challenge and Overview

One of the biggest challenges to the review process is that everybody dislikes it, both reviewer and reviewed. Some supervisors dislike giving positive feedback, preferring negative feedback because they themselves feel threatened, because they want to keep others in their place, or because they are engaged in political games within the company. Some dislike giving any kind of criticism, even constructive criticism, in order to avoid appearing negative. As the person being reviewed, you need to keep in mind that you have a part in this process and you must bring relevant information to your boss; you can't expect your boss to remember everything. Your boss is only likely to remember things that have happened over the past month or so. It's up to you to keep track of what happened throughout the year and to be ready to illustrate your accomplishments for your boss.

Approach your review by understanding the expectations and goals of the organization and of the reviewer, and then setting yourself realistic expectations. It's valuable to see yourself in partnership with your supervisor, and to consider your review as tied in to your supervisor's goals. Think of your review as designed to make your supervisor look great. You should look for the company to confirm that your actions are aligned with the company's goals. One of the questions you may ask is, "How do I determine everyone's goals?" If you are already employed, this can be done at any time. It might tie into a discussion of a merger, sales goals, or bonus plans. If you're engaged in the job search process, you may want to use the initial discovery process as a way to understand how the company evaluates the success of its employees, the key factors in annual reviews, and how often the company performs annual reviews.

Negotiating room during annual reviews depends largely upon a company's culture; some are willing to negotiate, others are less flexible. Some companies have very strict salary grades where employees fit into a rigid matrix. Once you're in a slot, you may well be in an established track that has a clear salary path or structure.

It's important to note that annual reviews can sometimes be confrontational because they involve discussions of salary, raises, and compensation. All employees want to get good reviews from their bosses, but we often do not know the supervisor's perspective and mandate. In addition, depending on the company's culture and procedures, certain financial aspects are preset in advance. Essentially, the manager is in a bind, and can't always agree with the employee's perspective.

The goal of an executive going into an annual review should be to focus on mutual accountability, not money. The review should focus first on your effectiveness in contributing to the team and how successful you were in meeting your deliverables, then on what you can do to improve.

◆ Preparation

Negotiating salary requires both advance thought and tact. Taking too aggressive a position may win you the battle, by gaining you a point on the appraisal, but lose you the war, if your supervisor is annoyed by your confrontation. Always keep your manager's perspective in mind. He or she may have some flexibility, or may be bound by someone else's strict guidelines.

The element most often missing in evaluations is a clear standard of measurement. Every objective can lead to a discussion of the criteria for success. If you're unclear about what constitutes success, or if you define success for yourself without others' agreement, the result can be a misalignment between your definition of success and your boss's definition. Managers often don't know how to set smart objectives, and it's important for you to help define the measurement framework by setting objectives that both you and your boss agree to.

Example: NetCareer Inc., a career coaching and consulting company, had certain goals for the year 2001. The first goal was to launch its Web site, the second was to secure several widely recognized author partners for providing content, and the third was to secure some corporate job coaches. The manager told the team, "Your goal is to identify and secure coaches to work with the customers who visit our Web site." One team member signed up ten coaches, and thought he had done a great job. However, the manager told that member that he had been expected to sign up twenty coaches. Another team member signed up twenty coaches, but she also failed to meet the manager's expectations: He had wanted her to sign up ten coaches with union experience, five with engineering experience, and five with sales experience. The sales team members all thought they had met their goals, but their manager didn't agree.

The problem in this example is misaligned goals. When the manager gave his team their instructions, he gave them vague objectives that were easy to misinterpret. The more specific your goals and objectives are, the easier it is to be sure everyone is on the same track. It's important to have ongoing reviews, both formal and informal, where you're being measured against your objectives and milestones. That way, if your goals and your boss's goals are misaligned, you can realign your objectives early on.

If you're doing well, then it's valuable to discuss your success with your boss and to be able to share your successes with co-workers. Similarly, if you're experiencing problems, it's better to discuss where the problems lie, to talk them over, and to take joint ownership. If you're able to take responsibility for your actions and share how you are doing according to your predefined goals, then each quarter you can have an informal discussion about your performance. Both you and your boss should be familiar with how you are doing and how that is aligned with the company's current goals and objectives. Then, if something happens and goals need to change midyear, there are no surprises on either side.

Performance goals should also reflect the changing dynamics of the company. The goals and objectives you define in your annual review should not be static. The fairest way of doing this is to base goals on performance or results, which takes the reality of the situation into account.

> ***Example:*** Johanna Ruddy was a sales executive at Intelligent Work Systems, with a sales goal for the year of $1 million. Intelligent had several small clients and one major client, Behemoth Buyers. Just after the end of the first quarter, Behemoth suddenly collapsed, creating turmoil in that whole sector of the industry. While working with the rest of the team to develop a new company strategy that didn't involve Behemoth, Johanna also met separately with her manager to rework her goals for the year. With Behemoth gone, it was no longer appropriate to hold her to her $1 million sales goal.

The first thing to keep in mind before going into an annual review is to be well prepared. Reflect on what your manager wanted from you this year. Sales are easy to measure, since they have established quotas, and your contribution to the company, either as an individual or as part of a team, is clear. If you are on a team that does not involve sales, be aware of your manager's goals, and be prepared to articulate how you contributed to his or her achieving the overall goals for the department. Success may be measured by an increase in productivity, or an improvement in the bottom line. As long as the objectives are clear and predefined, are objective, not subjective, and are mutually agreed to by both the executive and the manager, the requirements of the job can be measured.

Your focal point should be what you have done over and above the call of duty. Your job description is your average. Meeting expectations is understood. Most employees strive to exceed preestablished goals, to be innovative and creative. If you are in sales, did you sail past your quota? If you're in a non-sales area, did you affect the bottom line in some way, or achieve a gain in productivity or a significant expense reduction? You want to show the reviewer how you added overall value to your department and to the company as a whole.

An ideal place to start is at the beginning of the year, when expectations are set. This doesn't always happen, but it helps to understand your manager's expectations from the beginning. One effective way to accomplish this is to write down what you think the expectations are and hand this written assessment to your boss, saying, in effect, "This is my understanding of what you want me to do this year." Use this discussion to make sure your expectations are in line with your boss's. Then get your manager to buy into your understanding of the expectations.

If you didn't do this at the beginning of the year, or when you started the job, it should be done at the time of your review. There should always be clear communication and dialogue when the expectations for your performance, and the measurements that will be applied to it, are being established.

The more you can show your boss in black and white, the better. You might want to revisit your goals and objectives from your previous annual review. To what extent have you met or exceeded those goals? Document and record all your accomplishments through the year, and link your actions with the goals you have achieved.

Think of your review as a career development negotiation. The process would be a great experience if you received nothing but approval, but that isn't realistic. The review is an opportunity to learn and grow. By going in with an open mind and taking the criticism as something constructive, you will be more apt to listen, instead of becoming hostile, defensive, or frustrated. If you can see the other person's point of view, and perhaps even agree with some of the things he or she has to say, you can ask your manager for ideas for ways to make changes that will result in your growth.

The key is to build non-adversarial relationships with your coworkers, even when discussing yourself.

The bottom line is that employees need to empower themselves and say, "This is what I expect from you, the company or manager. This is where I stand and where my work stands." The employee needs to stand up for him- or herself and should state it as a benefit to the employer. Position such statements positively, as "I want to learn and grow, and the only way to do it is through valuable input from you [my manager]. How can we arrange this so that you and I are working together and have a partnership together?"

◆ The Negotiation

If done right, an annual review leaves the employee feeling reenergized—even if he or she didn't get a great review. This happens when the manager is open and articulates specific points that could be improved upon and the employee can move past feeling threatened to being able to accept feedback. It is helpful to go into your review with an open feeling, knowing your contributions, while avoiding confrontation. If you come into your review with a free-agent feeling, you'll project greater confidence. This mind-set will affect the whole process and it will make this a more constructive experience. This is your opportunity to remarket yourself. Confrontation should play no part in the process; it will not further a mutual sharing of interests, and you take the chance of setting a bad dynamic between you and your boss.

Analysis

Consider your interests by doing a self-analysis focused on specific areas. You will need to develop answers to questions like these:

Key Questions

Self-Analysis

- What do I think will be said in the review?
- Am I concerned about anything that may come up?
- What are my career goals long-term?

- What were my career goals for the preceding review period?
- What did I do to achieve these goals?
- What were my major accomplishments during the review period?
- Can I provide documentation or other corroboration of each of these accomplishments?
- What have I done to contribute to the success of my department? Of the company as a whole?
- Overall, what are my greatest strengths?
- What areas could I improve in?

Work Skills

- Have I demonstrated a complete knowledge of my own job, and an understanding of jobs that relate to mine?
- Do I plan, prioritize, and organize my work efficiently and effectively?
- Do I complete an appropriate amount of work, in a prompt and timely manner?
- Have I clearly demonstrated reliability, conscientiousness, and commitment to my responsibilities?
- Have I shown that I can plan, organize, and act in changing conditions?
- Do I present a positive attitude in my work and toward fellow employees and clients?

Communication Skills

- Do I communicate clearly, both orally and in writing?
- Can I explain a complex topic in a way that is easy to understand?
- Do I keep both managers and staff informed?

Supervisory/Leadership Skills

- Have I demonstrated effective supervision and management skills, including the ability to delegate responsibility and authority and to promote participation by co-workers?

- Have I demonstrated effective problem-solving and decision-making skills, including analyzing problems, identifying key issues, identifying alternatives, and making decisions in a timely fashion?
- Have I demonstrated an awareness of costs and an ability to use resources in a way that minimizes cost and maximizes output?
- Have I shown that I can accurately forecast and adhere to financial figures, and that I can carefully monitor expenditures?
- Have I clearly demonstrated leadership skills?

Planning

Use planning to establish your strategy, understand the other party's interests, and determine what options or alternatives would be acceptable outcomes. Ask yourself questions like these as part of your planning process:

Key Questions

- What do I want to achieve during my performance review?
- Do I view it as an opportunity to raise issues of concern with my manager? If so, what issues would I raise?
- How would I rate myself in each of the areas listed above?
- How is my manager likely to rate me?
- If there is a discrepancy between my own rating and the rating I expect from my manager, why does this discrepancy exist? What can I do to bring the two perceptions into alignment?
- How have I met the goals and objectives of my job description?

- What measurable accomplishments have I achieved during this review period?
- What documentation or other corroboration do I have to demonstrate my accomplishments?
- What tools, training, or other resources would help me do my job better?

Discussion

During the negotiation, you can get new information in two ways: through questions you ask, and through unsolicited information shared as part of the discussion. These are some of the questions you should ask and information you should listen for:

Questions to Ask

- These were the goals as I understood them. Do you see anything differently?
- How can we reach consensus on the job objectives and performance criteria and ratings?
- What, specifically, can I do to improve performance?
- What will you and the company provide to support me in improving performance (additional staff, training, information technology, etc.)?

Information to Listen For

- Clarity of performance objectives and agreement on the goals to be achieved during the review period
- The reviewer's recognition of the contributions you've made and your demonstrated accomplishments on the job
- The objective criteria being discussed (your performance goals) as distinct from the reviewer's personal interests or communication style. In performance reviews especially, it's critical to separate the person (and any personality conflicts you may have with him or her) from the content of what he or she is saying.

- Challenges the employer continues to face (e.g., declining revenues, rapid growth, potential acquisition target, department restructuring). Use these clues to understand the motivations of the employer and the reviewer. Recognize these challenges in setting goals for the next review period.

◆ Outcome: Next Steps

Most companies have a process and a written evaluation before the review. As part of the process, it's important for you to gain insight about yourself while validating your contributions, looking toward how you might be challenged by your involvements in future projects or roles within the company. Listen for what would be valuable for the employer as well.

Varied outcomes include an increase in salary, bonuses, and benefits. Raises are largely based upon a company's culture, and it's necessary to do considerable investigative work before your evaluation. Take this opportunity as a way to network and continue to build a relationship with your manager. Successful intracompany networking leads to the company having increased confidence in you, which leads to your being given bigger projects. It's important to remember that the confidence an employer has in you is based on what you have clearly accomplished.

Executive's Insight: Annual Reviews

Jeffrey Clegg, an accountant and attorney, is senior manager in the tax department of a major professional services firm. Here, he talks about his approach to the annual review process. The win–win principles exemplified in this excerpt are shown in the right-hand margin of the text.

"We receive evaluations twice a year, and then there's a once-a-year compensation process in which they take into account the midyear and the year-end reviews. You are evaluated on a pretty complicated scale and set of standards.

"The midyear review is geared toward letting you know where things stand, and letting you know about any areas where development is needed. The year-end review is very much the most important one. Our year ends May 31, and compensation reviews take place at that time, with raises becoming effective September 1.

"When I joined the company, I asked who would be reviewing me, how I would be judged, and by what standards. The answer was that I would be evaluated in several basic areas, including serving clients, technical skills, managing engagements, and business development. There's a manual that lays out all the standards for the various levels and how they should be rated, based on performance. The process is sometimes fairly subjective, but they have tried to take as much of the subjectivity out of it as possible, and for the most part it works fairly well.

Principles in Action: Identify the details.

"I asked about the review process during the interview because I wanted to be sure that I understood the criteria I was going to be judged against. Obviously, the evaluations are the basis for compensation and promotion, and so I wanted to be aware of how they would judge me.

Principles in Action: Identify objective criteria.

"My preparation for the annual review begins the day after the last review. I try to collect data that I know are important to the firm, like the number of client service hours that I've worked on, the financial data that I'm responsible for. I track those types of data all year long. I also keep a separate list of all my achievements, including those in intangible areas, such as mentoring people who are working with me, or getting articles published that add to my status within the field. I put all those things down on a list so that at the end of the year I don't need to worry that I've forgotten something.

"I spend a couple of hours a month making sure all my data are together. Then, at the end of the year, I spend a couple of hours summing it up and then present it to my boss for discussion. The actual discussion part of the review takes about half a day to go through all the information. In a big organization, it's particularly important to be proactive about your career in terms of raises, promotions, whatever. Being able to show what I've done over the year is a big help in terms of demonstrating my achievements and showing what I can contribute.

"In terms of raises, the criteria are both objective and subjective. Clearly, they look at the hard financial data, but they also look at the intangibles, such as mentoring. They try to factor it all in. Then the actual raise can range from as low as 5 or 6 percent for low performers to as high as 50 percent for the superstars.

"For me, the hardest part of the review process is getting constructive criticism. Some people perceive any kind of criticism as confrontational or something, so they don't want to tell you about areas where you need development. You have to drag it out of them. Your evaluations can't be perfect all the time. People want to be nice, and they want to be liked, but that doesn't really help me. I need to know the things I'm doing that are right, and I need to know the things that need to be worked on so I can continue to go up.

"I look at the review as an opportunity to advocate for career advancement. Everyone around here is busy; they have some awareness of what other people are doing, but they're certainly not focusing on that. At the annual review, there's a focus on 'What was Jeff's role in everything we've been doing?' I spend a lot of time preparing for my review. I go through everything I've done, and I think it pays off; I think I've been promoted more quickly and have done better on raises because of this.

Principles in Action: Focus on interests, not positions.

"Of course, I also do a lot of checking during the year. My boss and I have an hour-long check-in every two weeks, just to see what's been going on, the status of various projects, and so forth. At least once a month I ask him if there is anything I need to improve on, anything I need to do to make sure I'm satisfying his expectations. If anything is slipping, this is the best way to nip it in the bud; I don't want anything festering. You don't want a little thing to turn into a big thing; you want to be on top of the little things so they don't become a problem. I see people who just seem to want to sit at their desks and do their thing, but they're not communicating with their bosses, so the boss only sees the problems that arise, they don't see why it happened, they're not aware of the progress coming up to it, and they're not part of the plan to develop a solution to resolve it. If you only have a conversation when there's a disaster, that's bad. When that happens—when there isn't enough communication between executives and bosses—the bumps can become big issues. I want to be in there advocating for my career, not just letting it happen to me.

"Part of this is finding the best way to communicate with your boss. My boss is in Philadelphia, and he's a busy man. However, he has a long commute, and it's boring just driving, listening to the radio. I suggested that he call me then; I'm usually in the office late, and it's a good time to talk through things. We also use e-mail a lot, and voice mail. There have been times when we've had the equivalent of hour-long conversations just through leaving messages on each other's voice mail. I'll call him and set something out, then he'll leave me a message with his reactions, and I'll leave a message with my responses to that. If I just left a message saying, 'I need to talk to you about something that's come up, please call me when you have time to talk,' it would be much harder to connect.

Principles in Action: Invent options for mutual gain.

"If you're looking for a promotion, or a raise, always let the decision makers know as early as possible so you get it on their radar screens. I tell the people I mentor, if you want to get promoted in September, then by March, you had better be talking with your boss about what it will take to get you there. That way you have half a year to work on whatever you need to do to get to the next level. If you spring it on your boss at the last minute, there's not a lot of flexibility.

"Then, when you go into the review, treat it as selling yourself. Say, 'Listen, I deserve this. Look at the hours I work, the commitment I show. I've never missed a deadline. Clients love me, and that's what drives everything.' There will always be issues that arise, where something didn't go well, but if you're committed and flexible, they can't argue with you.

"Again, the key is communication. Keep track of your accomplishments, and let other people know about them. Say I got a call from a client saying, 'We just signed the engagement letter on a $5 million project,' you can bet I'm going to forward that to people. They will be fired up about that. Don't be afraid to communicate. Let your boss know that you want to be promoted, let them know what you expect. You have a one-to-one relationship with your manager, but your manager has a one-to-many relationship with the people he or she supervises. Your manager isn't going to be looking out for your career development. It's up to you to say 'This is what I want, help me get there and I will help you achieve your goals.'

Principles in Action: Communicate clearly.

"In the actual negotiating process, remember: Don't negotiate against yourself. Say you want a 30 percent raise. Some people will say in their minds, 'I'll never get that,' so they ask for 10. They do get the 10, but they could have had 15. Be aggressive. Ask for what you want. If you don't ask for it, you'll never get anything. Sometimes you'll get rejected—but sometimes you won't."

Chapter Summary: Annual Reviews

- **Be well prepared.** Document and record all your accomplishments throughout the year, and link your actions with the goals you have achieved.
- **Illustrate your successes.** Your boss is likely to remember only things that have happened over the past month. Communicate successes that were above and beyond the call of duty.
- **See yourself in partnership with your manager.** Consider your review as tied into your manager's goals and con-

firm that your actions are aligned with the company's goals.

- **Go in with an open mind.** Think of your review as an opportunity to learn and grow. If you view criticism as constructive, you will be more apt to listen, instead of being defensive or frustrated.
- **Focus on mutual accountability, not money**. Concentrate on your effectiveness in contributing to the team and how successful you were in meeting your deliverables. Think about what you can do to improve your efforts as part of your overall career migration path.
- **Bottom line—empower yourself.** Stand up for yourself in terms of the input you need from your manager. You should state it as a benefit to the employer. A statement such as "I want to learn and grow; how can we arrange this so we're working together for the same goals?" will go a long way.

PART THREE

The Big Picture

CHAPTER THIRTEEN

Professionals' Perspectives on Negotiations

I've always mainly relied on two things: the power of persuasion and convincing argumentation, and intuition.
—Ambassador Charlene Barshefsky,
U.S. Trade Representative

◆ The Big Picture

In order to be successful in your career, you need to be prepared for the multiple day-to-day negotiations that working with others requires. In this section, we're going to explore the challenges, significance, and importance of interacting with other people.

For the first part of this section, we have compiled interviews with two highly visible individuals, Ambassador Charlene Barshefsky and Tom Wheeler, who have diverse insights into the general negotiations process. In the second part, we provide a case study of the challenges associated with interdepartmental communications.

In the interviews with Ambassador Barshefsky and Tom Wheeler, you'll gain greater insight into their perspectives and personal negotiation styles. Whether it's navigating through sensitive trade negotiations or completing merger and acquisition negotiations, they use similar negotiation processes and approaches to dealing with people.

Ambassador Barshefsky describes her approach to negotiation as relying on two things, the power of persuasion and intuition. Her perspective is that negotiation is a give-and-take where you hope to "give less and take more," but it's a back-and-forth process: "You lay out your points and the other side responds, lays out their points in a fairly even tempo, sometimes punctuated by a little drama here and there." Barshefsky also explores the five key characteristics of a successful negotiator as: (1) knowing what you want and what you need; (2) persistence; (3) a good eye, as the body speaks volumes before the mouth ever opens; (4) agility, knowing when to readjust; and (5) the ability to see both sides of a situation.

Tom Wheeler declares, "The first thing that comes to mind in any negotiation is listening." He identifies three important traits for success in negotiations: discipline, persistence, and listening. Negotiation is a mutual process, a two-way street. In order to participate, he maintains, "you've got to be listening; it's not a bring-it-all-to-me kind of game." In addition, Wheeler recognizes that every day is a negotiation; you're constantly negotiating with your co-workers. With each discussion, you're building on existing relationships, whether the negotiation is over substantive issues or the implementation of those concepts. Wheeler also explores the impact of emotions in negotiations. He notes that "emotions will work against you every time; since one of the three most important aspects of negotiations is discipline, you've got to have discipline in terms of coming out of your chair."

◆ Ambassador Charlene Barshefsky

From 1997 to 2000, Ambassador Charlene Barshefsky was the twelfth United States Trade Representative (USTR). As USTR, she was a Cabinet member and the president's chief trade advisor and negotiator. The office of the USTR is responsible for developing U.S. international trade policy and leading or directing U.S. negotiations with other countries. While Barshefsky was USTR, her office negotiated more than 300 trade agreements and coordinated passage of nearly 50 pieces of trade legislation. Summing up Barshefsky's tenure as USTR, President Clinton described her as "a brilliant negotiator for our country."

When did you first become interested in negotiation?

Well, I was in law practice for many years, and in the context of law practice, one is often called upon to negotiate any one of a number of different kinds of things. My real interest in negotiations as a process began when I became deputy U.S. trade representative in 1993, and then of course ultimately the trade representative. At that point I became interested not just in the substance of negotiating—which, in the trade field, is very interesting—but also in the process of negotiation, the tricks of the trade, the kinds of things you learn over time when you literally do hundreds of these things.

And how did you go about refining that or determining the process that you would use? Did you use any kind of academic approach, a learned approach, as the basis for your process?

No. I've always mainly relied on two things: the power of persuasion and convincing argumentation, and intuition.

What would be the first words that come to mind when you think of negotiations?

I usually think of it as give-and-take. You obviously hope to give less and take more, and the other side hopes to give less and take more, but it is absolutely a give-and-take, back-and-forth, back-and-forth. You lay out your points, the other side responds, lays out their points. You respond—up and back, up and back—in a relatively even tempo. It's sometimes punctuated by a little drama here and there, but generally it's serious, workmanlike, short on histrionics.

The other word that comes to mind is "agility." There is no substitute for being agile, for knowing how to readjust, for knowing when it's time for some wholly new line of argumentation. A lot of that is intuitive. You just watch the other side. Sometimes you just know you're not breaking through no matter what they say. They can be nodding their heads in agreement, but you say to yourself, "They don't believe this at all." So agility—mental agility—is key.

How would you define a successful negotiator in general, the skills that they should possess, whether it's dealing with a trade negotiation or a career negotiation?

Well, you have to know what you want. This sounds self-evident, but you would be surprised at how many people go into a negotiation not fully understanding what they want. You also have to know what you need, which is different from what you want. You know, we all want the sky, but we don't need the sky. You have to know what you need, your bottom line, because the play in the negotiation is between what you need and what you want. If you get less than you need, you failed. You need to be willing to walk away if you don't get what you need. If you can't conceive of walking away, then your hurdle rate is very low.

You also have to be persistent. You can be the most agile negotiator in the world, but if you lose interest, you lose out. Persistence is very important. It's also important to have a good eye. The body speaks volumes before the mouth ever opens. You watch the other side, you just watch for body movements, you watch for expression, you watch for body language. Body language is a greater indicator than anything the other side will initially say. And, of course, you have to be agile. You have to know when to readjust.

In terms of the substance of the negotiation, the most important skill is being able to see both sides. The negotiation is not a one-way affair. You've got to be able to appreciate the arguments and the views of the other side. You may disagree, you may respond however you wish to respond, but you've got to understand their point of view. What's real to them is real to them, just as what's real to you is real to you. Because at the end of the day, if a negotiation can't be characterized as win–win, you're not going to reach "yes." At the end of the day, everybody has got to be convinced they came out of it OK.

In general, what do you see as the biggest challenges in negotiations?

The hardest part is developing a clear awareness of what you have to have. It's easy to be aware of what you want, but what you need is harder. That's because human beings are flexible, and tend to rationalize. You can persuade yourself you never really needed this or that. You say, 'No, it's all right, we don't have to have this, we don't have to have that,' but before too long, you don't have too much left. You have to pick your battles carefully. It goes back to truly knowing what you need, what is it that you need to have out of this. If you say to yourself, 'There is no way I'm walking away from these talks, I've got to get something,' then you have set a very, very low hurdle rate for yourself. The other side will quickly realize this, which sets you up for failure.

What is your overall strategy in negotiating?

I tend to try to be pleasant and respectful, and to be a highly substantive negotiator in terms of details and argumentation and trying to lay out a logical chain of thought. This is effective not only because it's clear, but also because it helps to keep the other side from taking offense; you're presenting a coherent view of the problem and the proposed solution. I've always used humor in negotiations, and that can be very disarming. It brings down the barriers and makes the whole process more human. I think I've always been good at forming relationships with the other side, so I tend to present a fairly consistent front. Now, that doesn't mean that one should be insensitive to the other person's predilection. You have to know something about the person on the other side of the table and you may need to adjust, but I don't presume it going in.

Have you ever encountered a situation where you've maintained your consistency in terms of your approach, but you have reached an impasse because of cultural barriers?

Not really, but you have to remember that my situation was very unique: I was negotiating on behalf of the United States of America. My experience in the process of negotiation is probably quite akin to the normal negotiation of a CEO, but when you're dealing government to government, people usually tend to get back to the table.

Do you think men and women tend to negotiate differently?

You know, I don't think there's any one thing that applies to each and every negotiator. Some people generalize that women are more intuitive and watch body language more carefully than men, but there are male negotiators who are very perceptive, and there are female negotiators who are absolute blockheads when it comes to interpersonal relations or intuition. I think probably women tend to be somewhat more sensitive to what's unspoken, as opposed to what's spoken, and I think that's extremely helpful.

Can you describe a situation where there was an impasse and you successfully redirected the discussion to achieve a mutually agreeable conclusion?

One of my favorites was an agreement we negotiated with China about intellectual property rights. We had been at the table until three in the morning, and the other side laid a proposal on the table that was simply not going to resolve any of the outstanding issues. At that stage of the proceedings, the outstanding issues were very complex, because the hard stuff is at the end. They put this proposal on the table and said 'Take it or leave it, this is it.' I just sat there, absolutely quiet for about 50 or 60 seconds—and in the context of a negotiation, at three in the morning, that's a long, long time. I said, 'If you are asking me to take it or leave it, the answer is obvious, I'll leave it, but I don't think you're asking me that. I think what you mean is you want me to take this back to my hotel room and study it and come back tomorrow.' I stood up, took the piece of paper with me, said, 'I'll see you at nine o'clock,' and left. There was silence on the other side, they were just stunned. I went back, looked at the proposal. It was not acceptable, but as in any proposal, you can usually find a little something to work with. I worked on it, came back, and we reached an agreement. I really think of this as an example of how important it is not to let a negotiation spiral out of control. When he said 'Take it or leave it,' if I had said 'This is a piece of trash, I can't imagine ever accepting it,' they would have gotten up and walked out. When you are presented with an ultimatum, or a tense situation, it's very important not to escalate. Sometimes that means humor, sometimes it means recharacterizing what you were just told in a way that gets everybody off the hook.

Is it ever OK to show emotions when negotiating?

Yes—but within reason. Some people are very dramatic negotiators, they pound the table, big booming voices, so on and so forth. It can be fun when you've got someone like that on the other side. I never found it effective. I've always found that being more workmanlike is more effective, in part because if you do reach a point where you are angry and want to show it, it's all the more effective because that is not the way in which you typically present yourself. There are some negotiations, not very many, where I thought the other side was being completely outrageous, and where I might have raised my voice or said 'This is a waste of my time,' but that's really rare. Because my usual style was well known, when it did happen, people would take notice. But it's not something I would do intentionally; intentional drama is rarely persuasive.

In general in negotiations, how do you know when not to push too far but to push just enough to achieve your objectives?

This goes back to a combination of persistence, intuition, and agility. How do you know when? You just know. But as you hammer away at issue A or issue B or X or Y, you just know when you reach a point that you can't go back to the issue, you just can't. You usually try to arrange the issues in such a way that you can go back persistently, but there's a point in every negotiation where there will be some issue the other side simply cannot budge on; even if the negotiator wanted to, he just can't, and there's just a point where you just know, you just sense it. But here's the trick of it: Then you have got to be able to reposition and try and present the issue in a way so totally different that it becomes a new issue. I've often said to people, 'You have to think about what you need, you have to think about what you want, and then you have to think about the 2,000 ways of getting there.' There are always multiple ways to get to where you want to go. Even if an issue drops out, there are often ways, in the context of other issues, to restore the balance in an agreement. This holds true whether you're negotiating trade with China or negotiating salary and compensation. There are ways of getting around it. You just have to be creative and agile.

Is there any area of negotiations you are still curious to explore and learn?

That's a hard question, because I suppose it's the old adage: practice makes perfect. There's no substitute for simply doing this kind of thing a lot. You just learn little things, little things about yourself, little things about your temperament; you learn about styles across the table, and sometimes that is incorporated into your own way of pursuing a particular issue in a negotiation. I think it's not that there is any particular technique or other. It's simply that each negotiation is different because the personalities are different and the issues are typically different. It's just a question of doing it.

What do you think is most valuable for people to learn about negotiations in general? What advice would you impart to others, whether from a career perspective or just in terms of building relationships and working with people?

I just think it goes back to what I said earlier, you just have to know what you want, what you are asking your boss for. Do you understand the constraints he or she may be under? Can you factor them in? And then it's being persistent, never in an offensive way. You have to watch carefully, because there is a line beyond which you don't want to go interpersonally, but persistence—letting that person know, "This issue is very important to me, and I need you to consider this issue, I need you to act on this issue in some appropriate way." Persistence of that sort is critical. You can't ever ask just once, and oftentimes not just twice. The other side needs to understand your need as much as you need to appreciate their potential constraint. You always need to be watching, because if you lose the interpersonal connection, you surely won't get what you want. You have to sometimes take a little bit of a risk, be a little bolder than you thought you could be, and if you watch carefully enough, nine times out of ten, you won't have crossed the line.

◆ Tom Wheeler

Thomas E. Wheeler is president and CEO of the Cellular Telecommunications & Internet Association and former president of the National Cable Television Association. Mr. Wheeler is an internationally recognized leader in telecommunications and has played an instrumental role in shaping its policy and technology over the last twenty years. As a telecommunications entrepreneur, Mr. Wheeler has been involved with numerous companies providing new cable, wireless, and video communications services.

What is the first thing that comes to mind when you think about job negotiations?

I think the first thing that comes to mind in any negotiation is listening, put on your ears and listen. In any negotiation, there are three important aspects. One is discipline, so that you are focused. Second is persistence. You need to hang in there, and that may be part of being disciplined. The third important aspect is listening, because people tell other people or signal to other people how they feel or how they could be best reached. A negotiation is mutual—it's a two-way street. You've got to be able to participate with the other person on his or her turf, and that means you've got to be listening. It's not a bring-it-all-to-me kind of game.

Do you have any negotiation techniques that you feel have been particularly effective?

There's one thing, a piece of advice that I give to people. I remember in my early days sitting down with my supervisor who would have an annual review, and say, "Well, this is what your salary is going to be for the next year." I would always say, "I'll take half of that and have a review in six months," and I always ended up doing better overall. I haven't really worried about the level of compensation once it gets beyond a threshold because I was confident I could improve it through performance.

What types of negotiations do you engage in on a daily or weekly basis?

Every day is a negotiation, and you're constantly negotiating with your senior staff. You hire strong-willed, capable people, and they are not just going to roll over and say,"Oh, yes, sir, you're the wisest person I've ever met." In an environment like the one I'm in, you are constantly negotiating with your customers, your clients, whether over substantive issues and the development of positions, or over implementation. When you run a diverse organization like this, everyone has a different perspective, and where they stand on issues depends on their perspectives. If you're a newcomer to the business, you have an entirely different view than that of someone who's been in it for years and years. Your goal is to try to find the common denominator that works for everybody.

And then there's the external life, dealing with policy makers or the media—it's a constant negotiation.

Has there ever been a time during a negotiation where someone's emotions have taken over?

Emotions can run high in a negotiation. But emotions will work against you every time in a negotiation. I said before that one of the issues is discipline; you've got to have discipline in terms of staying in control of yourself, in every way. It's a constant challenge because you are often dealing with important issues, you may be dealing with somebody's livelihood. I recently had a situation where someone was very irritated with something I had done, and I understood why he was upset. He wanted me to recant my position, but I refused to do that. We were both becoming agitated, and there was a real temptation to just blurt out what I was feeling—and I'm sure he had the same feeling. But both of us recognized that it didn't make a lot of sense to sit there and yell at each other or to say things that we would regret later. It's important to understand the other person's position, and to respect it—to be able to say, "I understand what you're saying. I can't agree with you, but I understand your point."

Some organizations seem to have problems with personalities getting in the way. What do you think is needed within the general corporate environment in terms of the way people interrelate?

I am an advocate of change, constant change. I sometimes feel that people who want to keep doing things the way we did them last year are using "that's the way it's always done" as an excuse for not thinking. The people who make it, in life and on the job, are the ones who have what I call a "healthy discontent." It's a fine line. You want to have a low threshold of discontent, the sense that "we could do better," while at the same time appreciating people's contribution in work. You want people to realize that that sense of things never being good enough isn't personal, but it's the people who get excited by that quest that you want to have around. And if you create that kind of environment, then a certain kind of self-selection takes place. People who don't want to be in that kind of environment will select themselves out. They'll find an environment that suits them better. We want people who know that just showing up is not 90 percent of the job. Still—and here's where the need to balance things comes in—we do things in life for positive results, in search of positive results. You can't have somebody constantly telling you negative things and be able to produce positive results. You can have a healthy discontent with the way things are, but it has to be a *healthy* discontent. By this I mean creating an environment that says that "OK" is not acceptable, you always need to be striving for "excellent," while at the same time rewarding people who do something really exceptional. The minute you stop growing, you've got to be out of there.

How do you think failure affects the individual, in negotiation and in overall development?

I can tell you all kinds of things that I wish would have been different. I've got a long list of failures that I wish had been different. They are all painful, but I'm not sure that they are not all without purpose, because they make you who you are. I'm a big believer in failure. I wrote a book called *Take Command: Leadership Lessons from the Civil War,* which examines how lessons learned in the Civil War battlefields are directly applicable to twenty-first-century business. The first chapter is "Dare to Fail." The next chapter is "If at First You Don't Succeed . . . So What?" Grant is the hero of that, because Grant failed at everything he tried, but he persisted and hung in there and ended up winning. That's really a key attribute. I've tanked companies. None of them have ever gone bankrupt, but I've taken some right down the tubes. Had some successes, too, and I think that there's a direct relationship between the two.

Sometimes a person can have a success in one situation, but be unable to replicate that success in other settings. Why do you think that might be?

It's not because they are incompetent, or because they were lucky the first time around. It's all the factors combined, the circumstances as a whole. I think there's also a challenge to keep hunger alive, keep discontent alive. Success has great burdens. It attempts to extinguish the flame of discontent, and that healthy discontent is really the driver. I'm writing a book right now called

Take Charge and Change. The first lesson of history is, "Change happens. Get over it." Your choice is, are you going to be active or passive in dealing with that? I believe the factor that decides whether you are going to be active or passive is your threshold of discontent. If you're comfortable, with a nice market share and a ton of cash, you may talk the game of change, but you don't have to do it. But if you're about to go under, you have to embrace change. You've got to say, "I'm not satisfied." It's like being in a relationship. You can love the other person but still say, "We can develop our relationship even further, we can bring things to a new level." At the same time, you don't want to devalue praise. If a person is constantly praising everything, then praise from that person loses its value. You want to know that praise from a certain quarter is a commodity to be cherished. Praise should be valuable, but not rare, and that's the judgment call. And, of course, the higher you move up the food chain, the less praise you get. As a CEO, no one says, "Hey, good job." You may know that you are doing a good job, but you are less likely to get that outside reinforcement.

On the subject of negotiations, did you ever have an experience where you felt that knowing more about how to negotiate would have helped?

My clearest memory of a negotiation was a long, drawn-out negotiation for software rights. It involved a number of transatlantic trips, lots of phone calls, lots of lawyers, and so on and so forth. We finally got the deal and went out for dinner to celebrate with the other team. Over dinner I said to their main guy, "Ed, what did you do before this?" This was really the first time I had reached out to Ed as an individual rather than as my opposite number in a negotiation. Ed replied, "I was a psychologist, specializing in physical behavior during negotiation." I said, "Do you mean to tell me that the whole time we were negotiating, you were reading my body language?" He said, "Yes." The lesson I learned from that was, I should have been listening to Ed. I shouldn't have been talking about software lines and codes, I should have been talking about him. Of course, he wouldn't have told me in advance that he specialized in reading body language, but the point is that I didn't even make the effort. In any negotiation, the most important thing you can do is listen. Turn on your ears.

CHAPTER FOURTEEN

Working in Groups

Every day is a negotiation. Your goal is to try to find the common denominator that works for everyone.

—Tom Wheeler, CEO, CTIA

◆ The Challenge and Overview

You've successfully negotiated your way through the hiring process and have gotten the job. Congratulations! But the negotiation process doesn't stop there. In most organizations, every day is a negotiation. Throughout your career, refining your negotiations skills is an evolutionary process; the more often you engage in collaborative negotiations, the better you'll become.

Once you've made the decision to take a particular job, it should be your goal to make the most of your time through effective time management, which can lead to maximized productivity. In order to do this, one of the most valuable skills you can develop is the ability to get things done in groups. Roger Fisher, of the Harvard Negotiation Project's Conflict Management Group, illustrates a four-stage approach for getting things done in groups that encompasses what he calls "the 4 Ps":

- *Purpose:* Know and explicitly communicate your purpose.
- *Product:* Envision the desired product of a successful meeting, and communicate that vision at the outset of the meeting.

- *People:* Invite key people to the meeting based on desired purpose and product.
- *Process:* Create and follow appropriate procedural ground rules.

This structured approach is designed not to make meetings more bureaucratic, but to make them more efficient. By adhering to a process, you'll provide a dependable and familiar structure that will facilitate the timely, productive completion of projects by avoiding duplication of effort and misunderstandings due to lack of communication.

Case Study

In this chapter, we explore the group dynamics of how different departments and personalities interrelate in a corporate environment. In this real-life case study of a progressive software development company, we observe tension among co-workers and the challenges associated with faulty communication, finger-pointing, and misaligned interests.

The company in the case study is beginning its second phase development effort on a new product, but communication among the different departments is faulty. Before the research and development process gets underway, the three key departments—sales, development, and customer support—need to align their goals and objectives.

Through the case study, we see how one manager identifies the roots of the problem, then takes action to resolve the problems.

The People

Kelley Anderson, vice president, operations

John Canter, chief technical officer, development

Alex Foster, vice president, sales

Andy Soros, director, customer support

The Scenario

Software Systems, a small software company, is just starting the process of developing an upgrade to their primary software product, but there are dissenting views on what should be included in the next version. The development, customer support, and sales departments all have different opinions.

Alex Foster, the vice president of sales, joined the company six months ago. Alex has felt significant pressure to build the sales pipeline, but he keeps getting excuses from his team: The product is too expensive, they need a sales promotion, the company needs to spend more on marketing campaigns to generate leads. Concerned about his team's comments, Alex meets individually with each team member to collect information. After these meetings, he feels that he has a good handle on his team's perceptions. However, while he respects the sales team's position, he realizes that he needs to understand the perspectives of the developers and customer support, as well, so he decides to arrange meetings with the other departments.

Before talking to the technical team members, Alex met with John Canter, the chief technical officer, to discuss the problem the sales team is having selling the product. John was initially defensive. He's been with the company for six years and is very proud of the product he and his team have developed. Given the time and creative thinking they invested in it, John thinks the current pricing structure is appropriate, and can't see a reason for reducing the price. John also doesn't see the need to spend more on marketing; the product is so good, it practically markets itself. All that is needed is for Alex's team to let people know about it, and sales will take off.

Alex listened to John's comments in such a way that John knew his concerns had been heard. Rather than agreeing or disagreeing with John, Alex explained that he is concerned with increasing company sales, and in order to do that, he would like to have as much information as possible. Since the technical team developed the product Alex is trying to sell, he feels that they would be an excellent source of information. John agreed that his team knows more about the product than anyone else, and agreed to let Alex meet with his department.

Alex met individually with all the members of the development team, and listened closely to the grievances they shared. He then did the same thing with Andy Soros and the customer support reps. As a result of these conversations, and the comments he had heard from his own team, Alex realized that, before the problem could be solved, members of all three departments needed to be made aware of the other departments' perspectives on the issues.

Since Alex had only been with the company for six months, he realized that he needed someone else to facilitate the meeting. His criteria were someone who was not part of the current issue but was familiar with the company's history and procedures, and who was perceived by others within the company as competent and fair. With these criteria in mind, Alex approached Kelley Anderson, the VP of operations, aired his concerns, and asked Kelley to facilitate a meeting between development, sales, and customer support. This meeting would not only enable everyone involved with the product to share their perspectives on the problems they were facing, it should also help generate a game plan for dealing with the problems. Kelley immediately agreed, saying that she shared his concerns, and felt that this was a step that the company needed to take. She promptly began to plan the meeting, deciding on the key people within each department who should be present and roughing out an agenda. Before the meeting actually took place, she contacted each department head and asked him to identify his team's main concerns, and to be ready to share those concerns with the rest of the group at the meeting.

Stage One Analysis

In his discussion with John, Alex followed the steps of any successful negotiation. John's comments about the sales team's inability to market a product that practically sells itself could have prompted Alex to defend his team; instead, he separated the people from the problem and focused on interests, not positions. Alex and John shared a common interest: increasing sales of the company's product. By keeping his focus on this mutual interest, Alex was able to keep the discussion on track.

Alex was also setting up one of the key components of the group process: People. In terms of the organizational structure, there was no need for Alex to check in with John before meeting with the technical team. By including John in the process at this stage, Alex demonstrated that he respected John's position, and involved him as part of the solution, rather than part of the problem. In addition, he was motivating key people who would ultimately be responsible for solving the problem.

In terms of the meeting that was now being scheduled, it met the criteria of the "4 Ps." The meeting had a clear *purpose*: to make sure that everyone involved with the product understood the perceptions and perspectives of others. Both Alex and Kelley envisioned a *product* for the meeting: a game plan for solving the company's internal disagreements about its software. The *people* at the meeting would be identified based on the purpose and product. And Kelley was already developing an agenda, which would set the stage for an appropriate meeting *process*.

The Meeting

Kelley wanted to include enough members of each department to make sure that different opinions would be heard. At the same time, if all members of each department were present, the meeting would be unwieldy—besides interfering with the operation of the company. To balance these interests, she asked each department head to come to the meeting with three members of his department. Thus, those present included Kelley herself, Alex and three members of the sales team, John and three members of the development team, and Andy and three members of the customer support team.

Kelley immediately set the tone and agenda for the meeting. She began by noting that there were a lot of exciting things going on at the company, and mentioned some recent highlights involving each of the three departments. This served both to set a positive, optimistic tone and to reiterate the idea that all three departments had a mutual interest—the company as a whole. She then discussed the agenda and framework for the meeting. She explained that all three departments shared one overall goal: to begin the design of the next major product release. However, before that could be accomplished, a variety of concerns needed to be addressed. She hoped that each person there would see himself or herself as part of the solution—not an easy challenge, but one that she had confidence they would be able to meet.

Kelley then opened the meeting by asking the key department heads—Alex Foster, VP of sales; John Canter, CTO; and Andy Soros, the director of customer support—to summarize the concerns of their departments.

Alex Foster, Sales

First of all, my people feel that installations are taking too long. When someone on the sales team makes a sale, they don't get paid until the installation is complete. Slow installations have an adverse effect on their income. It's frustrating to have done your part of the job but have to wait so long to be reimbursed for the work, and to have no control over the process.

Second, the sales team really needs a promotion to move the product and a marketing campaign to generate leads. Since the product is so complex—sometimes, incidentally, almost too complex for the customer to understand—following up on leads is a full-time commitment; it's impossible to also keep generating new leads, but new leads are the only way to grow the customer base, and the company.

However, even with a marketing campaign, it's hard to push sales when the team never knows when the product is coming out, and it's never on time. The sales team makes promises to clients based on the information we're given, but if that information isn't valid, then from the customer's perspective, it's the salespeople who are slipping in terms of timing, and this makes us look bad to our clients.

The members of the sales team make a real effort to present a professional image for the company, so it's frustrating to appear unreliable because we aren't given good information.

In terms of professionalism, some members of the sales team have also expressed the opinion that the customer support department does not always uphold the same professional image. In terms of dress, speech, and written communication, customer support tends to be more casual than sales. In and of itself, a casual approach is fine. However, the sales team works hard to present a certain image for the company, and this casual approach sometimes undermines that. This is exacerbated when people from customer support don't seem to be knowledgeable about their own product, or when they lack a core understanding of the industry.

In terms of customer support's interactions with the client, there can be communication problems. Sometimes, in their effort to help, customer support can overstep their boundaries. They make promises to clients, or offer to write extra reports, or get so caught up in a special request from a client—a request that deviates from the overall implementation plan—that they don't have time to do a good job on something else. When sales says one thing and customer support says another, the client ends up getting confused and frustrated. Also, a level of feedback seems to be missing. Sometimes customer support will be aware that a salesperson said something inaccurate, but this feedback never gets back to sales, so they can learn from their mistakes. The salesperson needs to be kept in the loop.

The sales team also feels that there are some problems in terms of product development. The development team doesn't seem to understand the industry very well. They don't know how the product needs to be positioned, and what can be done to make the product more competitive. In some cases, they have written code that is counterproductive to the point that it prevents a product from being sold. In other cases, they create something that's twice as complex as it needs to be. The complexity may have advantages, but it makes the product confusing to the client. The product has certain functions that don't have any perceived value in the market. Alternatively, sometimes the developers have come up with their own way of approaching a problem. That's all well and good, but within the industry, there are certain conventions in the way the information is displayed and processed. There are enough systems out there that have established the baseline on how data need to be presented. When our product doesn't present the data in that way, it's hard for the sales team to make the product attractive to the client.

Andy Soros, Customer Support

Well, I'm sure Alex was telling us what his people wanted him to hear, but that's not the way my team sees things. As far as we're concerned, the folks in development know exactly what they're supposed to be doing—and so do the people in customer support. It's sales that doesn't seem to know what they should do. I've heard more than one person say that the people in sales are focused on trying to make money, and their knowledge of the product is limited. It would really help if they would learn about the product in greater depth. It's customer support's role to know what the client wants on a detailed level, since the customer support team is on the front lines in terms of direct client contact. Unfortunately, sales doesn't communicate with customer support. They do things without notifying us, leaving us without key information. They also fail to follow company policies and procedures.

With respect to development, there is also a communication breakdown. Sometimes they will make major changes to a key feature or function, but won't let us know about the change. When this happens, we end up having to learn the new features on the fly, without any training. Our job is hard enough without having to work through features we have not been trained on while at the same time dealing with clients. We often feel that we're the ones getting passed over in terms of information sharing. It's hard enough as it is to keep up with the growth of the business. We can't hire good people fast enough, or provide full enough training, because the company is already eight weeks behind with implementations.

John Canter, Development

One problem that we see is that sales and development have two different ways of looking at the world. Developers are very detail-oriented. They tend to think in terms of problems that must be solved, seeing the negatives, if you will. People in sales tend to look at the issue more from the client's perspective. They'll say, "I have to have this feature, because my client needs it." But they don't see how that one feature fits into things from a development perspective. It may seem like one little thing, but that one little thing can affect dozens of other aspects and features of a project. At the same time, the developers need to realize that they're not just developing the product for the fun of it, but that the product has to generate revenue.

Development sometimes feels that sales is selling another product entirely—the current version, plus one. They should be a step behind, selling the product we've already completed, but they're always a step ahead. A logical development process involves having the sales team get the client's requirements, then pass those requirements on to development. Then development can design the product according to the client's needs. Yet in virtually any software company you hear the same complaints about development and sales. There is a disconnect, because neither area tends to understand what the other does. I'm not sure if this problem can ever be overcome, because the type of people who go into these fields tend to have such different mind-sets.

With regard to customer support, we find similar communication problems cropping up here. Customer support members come to development on an almost daily basis for all kinds of things, including daily product support. Whenever any kind of problem arises, we get immediate feedback or e-mail, or they think the problem is a bug and interrupt us to fix it. More often than not, it's a lack of understanding of a feature, not a problem with the software. Still, we're interrupted to deal with it, explain how to deal with it, whatever. We're trying hard to stay on schedule to avoid complaints from sales about late product release, but it's hard to keep on track when you're constantly being interrupted.

Stage Two Analysis

At this stage of the meeting, the most important element is *process:* creating and following appropriate procedural ground rules. Kelley has given each department head in turn the opportunity to share his team's perspective, and the other meeting participants have refrained from interrupting. Each department head has said some things that other participants might object to, or have a different take on. However, thanks in large part to Kelley's clear agenda and the collegial atmosphere she was at pains to institute from the beginning, no one has responded defensively.

As each department head spoke, Kelley recorded the department's key concerns on a whiteboard where everyone could see them. Again, she has refrained from comment, and has listed all the concerns, even those she might not agree with. Kelley is now ready to take the meeting to the next stage of development.

Kelley Anderson, Meeting Facilitator

OK, thanks to all of you for being so direct and honest with sharing your concerns and issues. The problems that I've listed here on the whiteboard concern all of us. Before we can move forward as a company, we need to address these problems—as a collaborative effort. If we all keep working separately, we're going to have interdepartmental warfare. What we need now is a constructive discussion as to how we can improve communication with other departments to make working together more efficient.

Stage Three Analysis

Kelley already had the purpose, people, and process. Now she is bringing the meeting around to focus on *product:* what the group is going to get out of the meeting. Kelley had participants break into smaller groups to address some of the concerns on the board, then share their solutions with the group as a whole. As these solutions were shared, Kelley again recorded them on a whiteboard. She broke the solutions into key communication breakdown areas—customer support to development; customer support to sales; development to sales; development to customer support; sales to customer support; sales to development. These were some of the ideas that surfaced:

Proposed Solution: Communication from Customer Support to Development

When we tell developers what to do, we should write the request out on paper, instead of relaying requests by phone or e-mail. This will reduce interruptions, and will also provide a record of the types of changes that clients request. We could schedule meetings between customer support and development—either biweekly or monthly—so we can categorize requests in terms of priority. This would enable us to feel as if we're being heard, as we do represent the client's needs because we're on the front line of customer service and installation.

Proposed Solution: Communication from Customer Support to Sales

If sales team members come to us in advance and engage us before making promises to clients, we get a better feel for what's going on in terms of prospective work. We also have clearer expectations as new clients come in, rather than being surprised all the time. On a subjective level, this kind of advance preparation would make customer support team members feel that their time is respected, and that they are seen as part of the overall company effort.

Proposed Solution: Communication from Development to Sales

We came into this meeting thinking that sales had no idea about what development does. It now seems that none of the departments are really clear about what the other departments do. It would be helpful to market the different departments to one another, so each department knows what all the others do. This would be bound to lead to better understanding. Also, in terms of development timelines, we produce an internal schedule tracking progress, which is updated weekly. As the schedule is updated, we could post it in a specified place—say, John Canter's door—so everyone can look at it. When there are slippages in development, it's not done deliberately to torture sales, it's something that can be beyond anyone's control. On the flip side, when sales meets a milestone, that gives us an important sense of closure. As a developer, you don't see the benefit of your work for months, even years; salespeople get a more immediate response to their work. Developers get excited when their products are sold, and we certainly want to make it as easy as possible for sales to do that.

Basically, we need to keep the communication channels open, in both directions. Development must say, "Here's what we're doing," and must give everyone the opportunity to give input and to buy into the product before we start designing it. We can't change things on the fly, so the more other areas understand how development works, the more smoothly the whole process will run. Building a schedule, sticking to it, and keeping the information flowing are all important to help us get rid of the feeling that we're working in a cave.

To help sales understand the development process, we think the sales team should be given some detailed training sessions. At the same time, we need to provide the salespeople with documentation in lay terms, terms that they—and their clients—can understand. We also need to tell the other departments up front what is planned for development, so that sales understands why development is taking a certain approach, why they are targeting a certain market, or why a certain feature is important.

Proposed Solution: Communication from Development to Customer Support

Even though development is the most technical department, it's important that we produce documents that are not overly technical in nature for customer support. Every two or three weeks, a training meeting should be scheduled, with representatives from each department. At these meetings, we can address customer support issues, or have a brainstorming session, or give sales a forum to voice their issues with regard to product development.

Proposed Solution: Communication from Sales to Customer Support

After the sales team makes a big-ticket sale, we need to hold a kickoff meeting with customer support. At that stage, both areas can agree on objectives in terms of time and what it will take to get the job done. If problems arise with implementation, we need a process where customer support can let sales know about the problems as soon as possible; this will help prevent further problems down the road. Instead of one group telling the other, "We need to do such-and-such," we need to set up a collaborative problem-solving process. If we can figure the problem out together, the solution is more likely to work for both groups.

Proposed Solution: Communication from Sales to Development

I think it would be helpful if we had a monthly meeting with the key managers. Then we could discuss where the product needs to be in order to be competitive. Developers could see what's important to salespeople, and why certain features and functions are important. We could come to a mutual understanding of time frames and technical challenges. From those meetings, we would develop an overall project plan that everyone could review in advance. Then, once a week, as part of our overall managers' meeting, we could touch base to see how it's going.

Also, it would be helpful to do a presentation on the industry as a whole for the entire company. This would result in everyone, company-wide, having a baseline understanding of the issues, why people are willing to pay $100K for our software, and the emotional and financial impact of a system. This would give both development and customer support a better read on what clients are looking for, and what we can expect to hear from them.

Stage Four Analysis

By now, the main work of the meeting had been achieved. The key *people* involved in the issue were all present. The *purposes* of the meeting had been to exchange information, decide on an action plan, and reach an agreement. The *products* included the notes made on the whiteboard for group use, individuals' notes for their personal use, and the final action plan. Throughout the meeting, the *process* kept things on track as the facilitator helped participants separate inventing from deciding, recorded ideas on the whiteboard, and guided participants away from such unhelpful avenues as point-scoring. Kelley kept everyone's focus on track at the beginning, which is the most difficult and sometimes unpleasant part of a meeting because there's a fine difference between a session to air concerns and a gripe session. When things got heated, her objective nature as a facilitator and her internal company jokes lightened the atmosphere. Also, by letting each department talk without interruption from the other, avoiding real-time bidirectional discussion, she was able to maintain the discussion flow, ensuring that the entire meeting did not extend beyond its scheduled two hours.

Outcome

There was a calm in the room after the two-hour meeting. Everyone felt better. Kelley noted that she had recorded everyone's feedback and solutions. Her next step would be to think about what everyone had said and come up with a game plan based on everyone's suggestions and comments. She acknowledged that she would probably have follow-up questions, but said that she would distribute her notes to those present to keep everyone on the same page. To keep the process moving, she suggested having the group reconvene in three days to develop an action plan for the next steps.

Final Analysis

By summing up as she did, Kelley completed the *process* for this meeting, but at the same time summarized plans and made assignments to keep the overall process moving forward. This summing-up also added to the *products* of the meeting: Kelley's list of questions for follow-up and the participants' assignments for the next meeting. This brought closure to many of the issues in the participants' minds, and the group forum allowed each to voice his or her concerns. Then, most importantly, Kelley's adept facilitation highlighted all the outstanding issues from each department's perspective using a whiteboard for all to see, then analyzed each department's concerns. By involving the various department heads and key people within each department, she was able to bring them into the discovery process, then move them to the collective problem-solving process. Once there was a clear plan of action, various individuals from different departments volunteered to work together to ensure more cohesiveness and interdepartmental communication as they moved forward.

Conclusions

As illustrated in this example, each participant in a group must use a variety of skills to bring the meeting to a successful conclusion: preparation and planning, active listening, understanding others' interests, self-control, analytical problem solving, clear communication, and focus. By using Roger Fisher's "4 P" approach, the different people and different perspectives involved in this problem could all be addressed. In any work setting that involves dissenting opinions, following a specific process can greatly increase the chances of success, both in collective problem solving and in terms of individual growth. Kelley's cool head and objectivity earned her the respect of the group, and showed why she deserved a leadership position within the company.

Embracing and practicing these techniques will allow you to collaborate better and work more efficiently and effectively with your co-workers, increasing your overall productivity within the company while simultaneously increasing your perceived stature. By developing, practicing, and applying these invaluable skills and techniques to any situation where there are differing opinions, you will significantly increase your chances of reaching a mutually beneficial or acceptable solution, time and time again.

Working in groups involves extensive negotiation, ranging from the give-and-take of everyday decisions to resolving differing perspectives on a strategic initiative. Use the following questions to understand Roger Fisher's "4 Ps:" Purpose, Product, People, and Process.

- Describe a problem you've experienced with a work team.
- Who was involved?
- What perspectives did each party have? What were their underlying interests? What positions did they take?
- How did each of you communicate your concerns?
- Did you involve an objective individual to facilitate the discussion?
- What came out of the negotiation? Were you able to overcome confrontation and agree upon a solution? How was this achieved?

Chapter Summary—Working in Groups*

Roger Fisher's "4 P" process. Apply a disciplined process that will facilitate the completion of collaborative group projects.

Purpose—Know and explicitly communicate your purpose.

- Understand all perceptions.
- Exchange information.
- Brainstorm ideas and options.
- Motivate key people.
- Decide on an action plan.
- Reach an agreement.

*Adapted from "Meeting Design: Getting Things Done in Groups," from the Harvard Negotiation Project's Conflict Management Group.

Product—Envision the desired product of a successful meeting; communicate that vision at the outset of the meeting.

- Notes for personal/group use
- List of questions to follow up on
- Draft memorandum for others
- Draft framework agreement
- Concrete action plan
- Get signoff from all participants
- Assignments for next meeting

People—Invite key people to the meeting based on desired purpose and product.

- Decisionmakers
- Clients/customers/constituents
- Internal experts and other functions
- Outside consultants/expert third parties

Process—Create and follow appropriate procedural ground rules.

- Assign roles:
  - Facilitator
  - Recorder
  - Timekeeper
  - Observer
- Formulate an agenda in advance.
- Prioritize order of agenda items.
- Allocate time for agenda items.
- Separate inventing from deciding.
- Record ideas on a flipchart.
- Revise the agenda, if appropriate.
- If appropriate, delegate gathering information or inventing options to a subcommittee.
- Avoid unhelpful ruts (e.g., point scoring).

- Have "closure" summarizing plans going forward and make assignments.
- "Choose to help."

APPENDIX

Putting It All to Use

The two model agreements included in this section have provisions that strongly favor the employer. Put your knowledge to use by identifying the undesirable clauses within the Employment Agreement and Options Agreement, then restructure each clause to bring the agreement back into balance from the executive's perspective. The numbers in the right-hand margin indicate each skewed clause, and correspond with the clause-by-clause analysis that follows each agreement.

Employment Agreement

THIS EMPLOYMENT AGREEMENT (the "Agreement"), made as of this ____ day of August, 2001, is entered into by and between Enterprise Systems, Inc., a Delaware corporation (the "Company") with its principal place of business at 1234 Technology Park, Suite 900, Boston, MA 02445, and ________________, residing at ______________________ (the "Executive").

The Company desires to employ the Executive, and the Executive desires to be employed by the Company upon the terms and conditions set forth in this Agreement. In consideration of the mutual covenants and promises contained herein, and other good and valuable consideration, the receipt and sufficiency of which are hereby acknowledged by the parties hereto, the parties agree as follows:

1. Term of Employment. The Company hereby agrees to employ the Executive, and the Executive hereby accepts employment with the Company, upon the terms set forth in this Agreement, for the period commencing September ___, 2001 (the "Commencement Date") and ending on August 31, 2004 (the "Termination Date"), 1

unless sooner terminated in accordance with the provisions of Section 4 (such period, as it may be extended, being referred to as the "Employment Period"). Upon expiration of the initial term, the Employment Period shall automatically extend for additional one-year terms, unless the Executive or the Company gives ninety (90) days' advance written notice to the other of its election not to extend the term.

2. Title; Capacity. The Executive shall serve and be employed as President and Chief Executive Officer of the Company and shall be based in the Boston, MA office. [2]

3. Compensation and Benefits.

3.1 Salary. Commencing on the Commencement Date the Company shall initially pay a base salary to the Executive at a rate of $155,000 per annum, with such salary being subject to annual increases and decreases by the Board (such base salary as in effect from time to time being referred to as the "Base Salary"). The Base Salary shall be paid in monthly installments, or in such other periodic method as is consistent with Company's standard payroll practice. [3]

3.2 Annual Company Performance Bonus. Between the Commencement Date and December 31, 2001, the Company shall pay to Executive an aggregate of $15,000 as refundable advances on the company performance bonus to be earned pursuant to this section (the "Company Performance Bonus"), paid ratably with Executive's regular pay (the "Bonus Advance"). The Bonus Advance shall be applied against any Company Performance Bonus earned during 2001. In the event that the Executive does not earn a Company Performance Bonus in an amount in excess of the Bonus Advance, the Executive shall reimburse the Company in an amount equal to the difference between the Bonus Advance and the Company Performance Bonus actually earned. The Executive shall earn annual bonuses as follows: [4]

a. for the year ended December 31, 2001, the Executive shall receive a Company Performance Bonus equal to one percent (1%) of (A) the Company's gross sales for the period starting on the Commencement Date and ending December 31, 2001 (calculated in accordance with generally accepted accounting principles as consistently applied by the Company) less (B) all returns, allowances and discounts applicable to or associated with such gross sales and less (C) any and all amounts paid to third parties for license and application fees (the net value of (A) less (B) and less (C) being referred to as "Company Net Sales");

b. for the year ended December 31, 2002, the Executive shall receive a Company Performance Bonus equal to one percent (1%) of the excess of Company Net Sales for 2002 over Company Net Sales for 2001;

c. for the year ended December 31, 2003, the Executive shall receive a Company Performance Bonus equal to one percent (1%) of the excess of Company Net Sales for 2003 over Company Net Sales for 2002; and

d. for the year ended December 31, 2004, the Executive shall receive a Company Performance Bonus equal to one percent (1%) of the excess of Company Net Sales for 2004 over Company Net Sales for 2003.

Such Company Performance Bonus shall be subject to Section 3.5 herein and shall be payable within 10 days after the distribution of the final audited financial statements.

3.3 Quarterly Bonus. For the remainder of 2001, the Executive shall be eligible to receive quarterly bonuses as follows:

a. if the Company achieves Company Net Sales of $234,735 for the fiscal quarter ended December 31, 2001, then the Executive shall receive a quarterly bonus for the second quarter of $5,000;

b. if the Company achieves Company Net Sales of $1,013,905 for the fiscal quarter ended March 31, 2002, then the Executive shall receive a quarterly bonus for the third quarter of $10,000; and

c. if the Company achieves Company Net Sales of $1, 278,125 for the fiscal quarter ended June 30, 2002 then the Executive shall receive a quarterly bonus for the fourth quarter of $10,000.

d. Notwithstanding the foregoing, if the Company achieves Company Net Sales of $2,972,210 for the three quarters ending June 30, 2002, but any of the individual quarterly targets were missed, the Executive will nevertheless receive all three quarterly bonuses for 1999, aggregating $25,000.

Such quarterly bonuses shall be payable within 30 days after the end of such fiscal quarter, and shall be subject to Section 3.5 herein. The Executive will be eligible to receive quarterly bonuses, similarly structured as in the 2001 plan, in the years subsequent to 2001. The quarterly bonuses will be structured based on business goals agreed to between the Executive and the Board at the discretion of the Board.

3.4 Annual Bonus. The Executive shall be eligible to receive an annual bonus for each calendar year for which the Company has net income, in an amount equal to 15% of the net income before taxes, as calculated in accordance with GAAP. Such annual bonus shall be subject to Section 3.5 herein and shall be payable within 10 days after the distribution of the final audited financial statements.

3.5 Compensation Cap. Notwithstanding anything to the contrary contained elsewhere in this Agreement, the salary and bonuses paid to the Executive pursuant to Sections 3.1, 3.2, 3.3, and 3.4 above, shall be subject to an aggregate compensation cap as follows:

a. $275,000 for fiscal years ended December 31, 2001 and 2002;

b. $300,000 for fiscal year ended December 31, 2003; and

c. $400,000 for fiscal year ended December 31, 2004.

3.6 Stock. Concurrently with the signing of this Agreement, the Company shall grant to the Executive 18,170 shares of the Company's common stock subject to a Stock Restriction Agreement in substantially the form attached hereto.

3.7 Stock Option. The Executive shall be entitled to participate in the Company's stock option plan, established or to be established by the Board or other such plan as created from time to time by the Board. Initially, the Executive shall be granted an option to purchase 72,680 shares of the Company's Common Stock. The terms and conditions of grant and exercise governing such option shall be as set forth in the form of Non-Qualified Stock Option Grant Agreement attached hereto as Exhibit B.

3.8 Fringe Benefits. The Executive shall be entitled to participate in all benefit programs that the Company establishes and makes available to its Executives, if any.

3.9 Vacation. The Executive shall be allowed three (3) weeks of paid vacation during each calendar year. In the event that the Executive does not use all vacation earned in a calendar year, the accrued but unused vacation allowance shall be forfeited.

3.10 Reimbursement of Expenses. The Company shall reimburse the Executive for all normal business expenses incurred or paid by the Executive in connection with, or related to, the performance of his duties, responsibilities or services under this Agreement, upon presentation by the Executive of documentation, expense statements, vouchers or such other supporting information as the Company may reasonably request. Such expenses shall be reimbursed on a semi-annual basis.

3.11 Health Insurance. For so long as the Company has an established health care plan, the Executive shall pay 100% of the premium for the Executive's participation in the Company's health care plan.

3.12 Company Policies and Procedures. Except as specifically provided herein to the contrary, the Executive shall be subject to all Company policies, procedures and practices generally applicable to Executives of the Company.

3.13 Relocation Allowance. The Company agrees to provide the Executive with a Relocation Allowance which will not exceed $________. The purpose for this Relocation Allowance is to reimburse the Executive for relocation expenses actually incurred. As such, the Executive shall be required to provide the Company with copies of receipts for all relocation expenses incurred. The Company shall reimburse the Executive for all such relocation expenses within 90 days of receipt of each receipt. For the purposes of this provision, relocation expenses shall be limited to actual moving, packing and unpacking expenses for all household goods.

9

4. Employment Termination. The employment of the Executive by the Company pursuant to this Agreement shall terminate upon the occurrence of any of the following:

4.1 Expiration of the Employment Period in accordance with Section 1;

4.2 At the election of the Company, for Cause (as defined below), immediately upon written notice by the Company to the Executive. For the purposes of this Section 4.2, "Cause" "means (i) the commission by Executive of a felony or a crime involving moral turpitude or the intentional commission of any other act or omission involving dishonesty or fraud with respect to the Company or any of their customers or suppliers, (ii) conduct by Executive tending to bring the Company into substantial public disgrace or disrepute not cured within ten (10) business days after written notice thereof, (iii) substantial and repeated failure by Executive to perform duties of the office held by Executive as reasonably directed by the Board not cured within ten (10) business days after written notice thereof, (iv) substantial and repeated poor performance by Executive of his duties as specified in written notice from the Board specifying such deficiencies and the required actions needed to cure such poor performance, and not cured within ten (10) business days after written notice thereof, (v) any material breach of this Agreement or the agreements attached hereto as Exhibits A, B and C, not cured within ten (10) business days after written notice thereof from the Company or (vi) the Company's general displeasure with the services provided by the Executive. The cure periods specified in this Section 4 shall not apply to any breach which by its nature is not susceptible to a cure.

10

4.3 Upon the death or thirty (30) days following the disability of the Executive. As used in this Agreement, the term "disability" shall mean the inability of the Executive, due to a physical or mental disability, for a period of 30 substantially consecutive days, to perform the essential functions of his position as Company President and Chief Executive Officer. A determination of disability shall be made by a physician satisfactory to both the Executive and the Company, provided that if the Executive and the Company do not agree on a physician, the

11

Executive and the Company shall each select a physician and these two together shall select a third physician, whose determination as to disability shall be binding on all parties;

4.4 At the election of the Executive, upon not less than sixty (60) days prior written notice of termination other than for a material breach of this Agreement by the Company; or

4.5 At the election of the Executive for a material breach of this Agreement by the Company, which such breach has not been cured within ten (10) business days after written notice thereof from the Executive.

5. Effect of Termination.

5.1 Termination for Cause or at Election of Executive. In the event the Executive's employment is terminated by the Company pursuant to Section 4.2 or by the Executive pursuant to Section 4.4, the Company shall pay to the Executive the compensation and benefits otherwise payable to him under Section 3 through the last day of his actual employment by the Company.

5.2 Termination for Death or Disability. If the Executive's employment is terminated by death or because of disability pursuant to Section 4.3, the Company shall pay to the estate of the Executive or to the Executive, as the case may be, the compensation which would otherwise be payable to the Executive up to the end of the month in which the termination of his employment because of death or disability occurs.

5.3 Termination by Company Other Than For Cause.

(a) If the Executive's employment is terminated by the Company other than for Cause as defined in Section 4.2, the Company shall pay to the Executive the compensation and benefits otherwise payable to him under Section 3 through the last day of his actual employment by the Company, and shall continue to pay his Base Salary at the rate then in effect for a period of two (2) weeks as severance pay.

12

(b) The Executive's rights with respect to the Executive's stock options in the event of termination shall be governed by the terms of the Incentive Stock Option Grant Agreement applicable thereto.

6. Assignment of Invention, Nondisclosure and Noncompetition Agreement.

13

(a) Confidential Information and Materials. The Executive agrees that all information and materials acquired by him concerning the Company's business and the Company's customers are confidential and shall not be disclosed to any other person or used in any way that would be detrimental to the Company's business or to the business of the Company's customers. Such confidential information and materials include, without limitation, all information and materials belonging to, used by, or in the possession of the Company or its customers relating to: Company financial information, business strategies, pricing, customers, customer patient information and medical records, technology, programs, costs, Executive compensation, marketing plans, developmental plans, computer programs, computer systems, inventions and trade secrets of every kind and character.

(b) New Developments. The Executive agrees that during the course of his employment with the Company, he will promptly disclose to the Company all improvements, inventions, discoveries, innovations, systems, techniques, ideas, processes, programs, and other things which may be of assistance to the Company in its development of services or products, and which were made or conceived by the Executive alone or with others, while employed by the Company, regardless of whether developed on working time or personal time or whether developed at the Company's offices or the Executive's home (collectively referred to hereinafter as "New Developments"). The Executive agrees that all New Developments are the sole and exclusive property of the Company. The Executive agrees, upon the request of the Company, to do all lawful things reasonably necessary to ensure the Company's ownership of such New Developments including, without limitation, the execution of any necessary documents assigning and transferring to the Company and its assigns all of his rights, title and interest in and to such New Developments.

(c) Surrender of Company Material Upon Separation. The Executive agrees that upon separation of his employment with the Company, he will immediately surrender to the Company all property belonging to the Company. The Executive also agrees to surrender to the Company all personal notes, drawings, manuals, documents, photographs or correspondence, including copies thereof, relating to any confidential information or New Developments which are in his possession or in the possession of an individual or entity under his control.

(d) Covenant Not To Compete.

A. While employed by the Company and for a period of twenty-four (24) months after the date of the Executive's separation from employment, the Executive shall not, within the United States, for himself or as an agent or Executive of any business enterprise, directly or indirectly, be engaged in any activity or business which directly or indirectly competes with the business of the Company. The business of the Company is defined as information technology throughout the global marketplace.

14

B. The Executive represents and warrants to the Company that his experience and abilities are such that he can obtain employment in a business different from the business conducted by the Company. The Executive further represents and warrants that he understands that the restrictions contained in this Section ("Covenant Not To Compete") apply regardless of whether Executive's separation from the Company is voluntary or involuntary or is with cause or without cause.

C. This Covenant Not To Compete shall not prohibit the ownership by the Executive of stock of any publicly-held corporation (as hereinafter defined) so long as such stock comprises less than one percent (1%) of the issued and outstanding stock of the same class of the issuing corporation. For purposes of this Subsection, the term "publicly-held corporation" means a corporation which is subject to the periodic reporting requirements of Section 12(g) of the Securities Exchange Act of 1934, as amended.

D. The Executive acknowledges that the activities prohibited and the geographic and time restrictions imposed by the provisions of this Covenant Not To Compete are fair and reasonable and are reasonably required for the protection of the Company's legitimate business interests. In the event that any part of this Covenant Not To Compete is held to be unenforceable or invalid, the parties agree that a court of competent jurisdiction will designate geographic and/or time restrictions or proscribed activities as is deemed reasonable and will thereupon enforce the covenants as modified. It is the intent of the parties that the nature of the restrictions, the geographic scope of the restrictions and the periods of time restrained be the maximum deemed to be fair and reasonable.

E. If, after separation of employment, the Executive violates this Covenant Not To Compete, the duration of this Covenant Not To Compete after separation of employment shall be computed from the date the Executive resumes compliance with this Covenant Not To Compete.

(e) Solicitation of Company Executives After Separation. The Executive agrees that, for a period of twenty-four (24) months after the separation of his employment with the Company, he will not, directly or indirectly (whether as a sole proprietor, partner, stockholder, director, officer, Executive or in any other capacity as principal or agent), do any of the following:

A. Hire, or attempt to hire for employment, in any business venture, any person who was an Executive of the Company or any subsidiary or parent of the Company within the six (6) month period immediately preceding the Executive's separation of employment with the Company, or attempt to influence any such person to terminate such employment; or

B. In any other manner interfere with, disrupt or attempt to disrupt the relationship, contractual or otherwise, between the Company or any subsidiary or parent of the Company and any of their Executives.

(f) Solicitation of Company Customers/Clients. The Executive agrees that, for a period of twenty-four (24) months after the separation of his employment with the Company, he will not, directly or indirectly (whether as a sole proprietor, partner, stockholder, director, officer, Executive or in any other capacity as principal or agent) solicit the business of any of the Company's customers/clients. For the purposes of this Agreement, the Company's customers/clients shall be defined as any customer/client for which the Company has provided services or prepared a bid or proposal to provide services within the twenty-four (24) month period immediately preceding the Executive's separation of employment with the Company.

The provisions of this Section 6 shall survive the termination of this Agreement.

7. Notices. All notices required or permitted under this Agreement shall be in writing and shall be deemed effective upon personal delivery (including by facsimile) or upon deposit in the United States Post Office, by registered or certified mail, postage prepaid, addressed to the other party at the address shown above, or at such other address or addresses as either party shall designate to the other in accordance with this Section 7.

8. Pronouns. Whenever the context may require, any pronouns used in this Agreement shall include the corresponding masculine, feminine or neuter forms, and the singular forms of nouns and pronouns shall include the plural, and vice versa.

9. Entire Agreement; Severability. This Agreement constitutes the entire agreement between the parties and supersedes all prior agreements and understandings, whether written or oral, relating to the subject matter of this Agreement. The Executive hereby agrees that each provision herein shall be treated as a separate and independent clause, and the unenforceability of any one clause shall in no way impair the enforceability of any of the other clauses herein. Moreover, if one or more of the provisions contained in this Agreement shall for any reason be held to be excessively broad as to scope, activity, subject or otherwise so as to be unenforceable at law, such provision or provisions shall be construed by the appropriate judicial body by limiting or reducing it or them, so as to be enforceable to the maximum extent compatible with the applicable law as it shall then appear.

10. Amendment; Waiver. This Agreement may be amended or modified only by a written instrument executed by both the Company and the Executive. Any waiver by the Company of a breach of any provision of this Agreement shall not operate or be construed as a waiver of any subsequent breach of such provision or any other provision hereof.

11. Governing Law; Arbitration. This Agreement shall be construed, interpreted and enforced in accordance with the laws of the Commonwealth of Massachu-setts. Any controversy, claim, or dispute arising out of or relating to this Agreement, or the breach thereof, or the termination thereof, including any claims under federal, state, or local law, shall be resolved by arbitration in Boston, Massachusetts, in accordance with the commercial arbitration rules of the American Arbitration Association. Any award rendered by the arbitrators shall be final and binding, and judgment upon the award may be entered in any court having jurisdiction thereof. In connection with any award, the arbitrators shall identify a "non-prevailing party." Such non-prevailing party shall be solely responsible for all costs charged by the American Arbitration Association or the arbitrators in connection with the arbitration, and the prevailing party shall be reimbursed for any amounts advanced therefor, including without limitation filing fees, arbitrators' fees, administrative fees, and out-of-pocket costs charged by the American Arbitration Association.

15

12. Successors and Assigns. This Agreement shall be binding upon and inure to the benefit of both parties and their respective successors and assigns, including any corporation with which or into which the Company may be merged or which may succeed to its assets or business, provided, however, that the obligations of the Executive are personal and shall not be assigned by him.

13. Miscellaneous.

13.1 No delay or omission by the Company in exercising any right under this Agreement shall operate as a waiver of that or any other right. A waiver or consent given by the Company on any one occasion shall be effective only in that instance and shall not be construed as a bar or waiver of any right on any other occasion.

13.2 The captions of the sections of this Agreement are for convenience of reference only and in no way define, limit or affect the scope or substance of any section of this Agreement.

13.3. The Executive represents and warrants that his performance of this Agreement and the agreements set forth in the Exhibits hereto will not breach any agreement entered into by him with a prior employer, including particularly those relating to confidentiality, trade secrets, proprietary information, and covenants not to compete or to solicit Executives.

IN WITNESS WHEREOF, the parties hereto have executed this Agreement as of the day and year set forth above.

Enterprise Systems, Inc.	Executive
By: ______________________	______________________
President & CEO	Signature

Analysis: Employment Agreement

1. **Undesirable Clause:** This is not necessarily an undesirable clause, as it is an important consideration for the executive. The key question you must ask yourself is, "Am I looking for more stability, or more flexibility?"
   Proposed Action: From the executive's perspective, the most desirable structure is to have an at-will contract with a long severance period. Then, if you're fired for any reason, you will be protected with an extended severance package. When you have a three-year contract, the company can only fire you "for cause"; you can quit, but you may be prohibited from working for anyone else for a certain period of time and without severance. Typically, the board of directors will seek a longer-term contract with a top-level executive because the board's interests are stability and consistency. The length of your employment contract really depends on your situation.

2. **Undesirable Clause:** The executive's duties and responsibilities are not clearly stated. In the event of a merger and a restructuring of the management team, or if the board of directors decides to materially change the position for the worse—for example, to reduce the executive's responsibilities, or negatively alter the position's title—the executive will have no leverage to exercise any severance clauses due to the material change in position.
   Proposed Action: Specifically define your duties and responsibilities so if your role substantially changes, you will have options. If you are a president and CEO, the language might read, "...shall have primary authority and responsibility, subject to the control of the Board, for operational control, strategic planning and implementation, and marketing for the Company. As President, the Executive shall initially

serve as a non-voting member of the Board until the next regularly scheduled election of directors, where he will stand for election as a full voting member of the Board."

3. **Undesirable Clause:** The executive's salary is subject to "...annual 'decreases' by the Board."
   Proposed Action: Remove the word 'decreases'; you joined the company based on certain base salary and overall compensation expectations. If the board decides to reduce your base pay, it may not be enough to meet your monthly financial obligations, it does not address your personal security issues, and is simply not the deal you negotiated when joining the company.

4. **Undesirable Clause:** Since the executive's bonus or advance is "refundable" it exposes him or her to a potential future liability. Also, if the executive does not earn a bonus amount in excess of the bonus advance, then he or she will have to reimburse the company in an amount equal to the difference between the bonus advance and the earned portion.
   Proposed Action: Request that the advance be nonrefundable because you consider this part of your base compensation. You might want to introduce objective criteria, stating, "based on the industry, company size, and position, my value is X, therefore, I cannot justify taking a step back in compensation at this point in my career. I am excited about the prospect of making a positive impact on the company's growth, but this is the bottom line of what I need in order to feel secure and make the significant commitment the position requires."

5. **Undesirable Clause:** The executive's stock options are nonqualified options (NSOs), rather than incentive stock options (ISOs). Because of tax implications, these are favorable to the employer and are a disadvantage to the executive.
   Proposed Action: Inquire about incentive stock options as opposed to nonqualified stock options, stating your tax concern that you will have to pay taxes in advance without having realized any cash gains.

6. **Undesirable Clause:** The executive's unused, but earned, vacation time in a calendar year shall be forfeited.
   Proposed Action: First, understand the company's vacation policy by reading their employment manual. Once you understand their policies, you might state, "I am making a significant time and energy

commitment to the company, the demands of which may not be conducive to vacations taken within a calendar year. To best fulfill this commitment, time with my family is important so that I can remain focused and effective at work"

7. **Undesirable Clause:** The executive will be reimbursed for expenses on a semi-annual basis.
   Proposed Action: It is not uncommon to see such long reimbursement time frames. You should negotiate two to four weeks reimbursement, upon submitting your expenses. You might be traveling extensively and incurring significant expenses, and the longer your reimbursement period, the greater personal liability you incur. Keep the reimbursement period as short as possible or arrange for the use of a company credit card for charging significant expenses.

8. **Undesirable Clause:** The executive is responsible for 100 percent of his or her personal and family's health insurance premium.
   Proposed Action: State that health insurance is obviously a critical part of your benefits package and you'd like the premium covered by the company. If it's a small company, you might want to negotiate a larger co-pay, such as having the company contribute 50 percent to 75 percent of the monthly cost.

9. **Undesirable Clause:** The company shall reimburse the executive for all expenses within ninety days of receiving each receipt. Also, if relocation involves selling a current house and purchasing a new one, there are no provisions to subsidize selling the home, closing costs, temporary housing, etc.
   Proposed Action: First, since you will most likely incur significant expenses for your move, you should request reimbursement within fifteen days of submitting your expenses to the company. Also, if it is applicable due to the distance of the relocation, you might want to consider negotiating the inclusion of transporting your automobile, expenses incurred in the sale of your home (including sales commissions and closing costs), and expenses incurred in the purchase of a new home, including closing costs and temporary housing costs for a period of no longer than a specified number of weeks.

10. **Undesirable Clause:** The most critical language in the employment termination section is that the executive can be terminated because of the company's "general displeasure with the services provided by the executive."

Proposed Action: Simply remove this phrase; it is too general and can refer to anything. It's crucial to be specific when defining "cause," and you should always be provided the opportunity to "cure" any poor performance claims the company maintains. Such a clause has the effect of nullifying the entire agreement, and does not provide the executive with employment security.

11. **Undesirable Clause:** If the executive needs to exercise his or her disability clause, thirty substantially consecutive days of failure to perform the essential functions is too short a time period. What if the executive is in a car accident or needs rehabilitative care that will take sixty days, and has had stellar performance? He or she should have a fair and reasonable period to recuperate.
Proposed Action: A reasonable time might be sixty to ninety days of consecutive failure to perform the essential functions. Generally, rehabilitation takes longer than thirty days. Most executives do not focus on this area, but you can never be too careful and it's important to anticipate all possible scenarios.

12. **Undesirable Clause:** If the executive is terminated for "non-cause," which basically means for any reason (i.e., change in ownership and management, or personality conflicts), the severance period is only two weeks. This is entirely too short since it would be virtually impossible to find a commensurate position in such a short period of time.
Proposed Action: For an executive, a minimum of six months is reasonable and you might negotiate as much as eighteen months, depending on your position. Rather than focusing on the negative reasons that you might be terminated, focus on the positive reason: if the company is acquired and the new owners want to bring in a new management team. You might say, "If this scenario happens, I want to protect myself from a material change in position."

13. **Undesirable Clause:** Ideally, the executive should avoid including a noncompete clause as part of the employment agreement. As it is currently written, the executive is restricted from working in his or her entire industry for twenty-four months. This is unreasonable because it prevents the executive from working in his or her area of expertise.
Proposed Action: It's wise to offer a nonsolicitation clause as an alternative to a noncompete as it truly protects the employer's interests. If they insist on you signing a noncompete, a viable solution is a buyout clause that states, if such restrictions are imposed, they need to pay

you a lump sum of $200,000 to activate your noncompete agreement, which would fairly compensate you for your absence from your core area of expertise.

14. **Undesirable Clause:** Remove the phrase "The business of the Company is defined as information technology throughout the global marketplace." If the executive leaves the company voluntarily or is terminated for any reason, he or she is essentially restricted from working in the entire information technology industry for two full years. If the executive's entire career has been built within that industry, this will unfairly prevent him or her from making a living.
Proposed Action: Rework the language to be more specific in terms of actual named competitors and more focused in terms of regions. In addition, a more reasonable time frame is one year, as opposed to two years. An alternative to the current phrasing might be, "The business of the Company is defined as medical billing and patient scheduling systems throughout the Northeast region of the U.S."

15. **Undesirable Clause:** Generally, arbitration clauses favor companies. However, arbitration clauses can also be advantageous to executives in certain circumstances. By agreeing to such a clause, the executive gives up his or her right to a jury trial in court, which is particularly desirable in any discrimination claim.
Proposed Action: The common-sense way to deal with an arbitration clause included as part of your employment agreement is to accept its presence. Disputing the clause may give the appearance that you are anticipating problems in the employment relationship. It's important to be aware that by accepting arbitration, you are giving up your rights to sue the employer in a court. The mere mention of this will mark you as a troublemaker. Before signing any legal document with an arbitration clause, make sure you understand what it means. Be careful about agreeing to a city or state where arbitration or litigation will take place, or agreeing to cover the legal expenses of the other party if you lose the case.

Nonqualified Stock Option Agreement

This NONQUALIFIED STOCK OPTION AGREEMENT (the "Agreement") is made and entered into as of the ____ day of ____________, 200__, by and between Enterprise Systems, Inc., a Delaware corporation (the "Corporation"), and ___________ (the "Executive").

WHEREAS, the Board of Directors of the Corporation has determined that it is in the best interests of the Corporation to grant the Executive a Nonqualified Stock Option under the Enterprise Systems, Inc. 2000 Stock Incentive Plan (the "Plan") and has authorized and directed the Corporation to grant a Nonqualified Stock Option to the Executive under the terms and conditions set forth in this Agreement;

NOW, THEREFORE, the Corporation and the Executive agree as follows:

1. <u>Grant of Nonqualified Stock Option.</u> The Executive is granted a Nonqualified Stock Option (the "Option") to purchase ten thousand (10,000) Shares.

2. <u>Exercise Price Per Share.</u> The exercise price of the Option granted under this Agreement is $1.00 per Share.

3. <u>Option Grant Date.</u> The Option Grant Date is __________, 2001.

4. <u>Employment Date.</u> The Executive's Employment Date is _________.

5. A. <u>Vesting Schedule.</u> The Option shall vest and become exercisable in accordance with the following schedule:

Period from Employment Date	Vested Percentage	Forfeited Percentage
Less than 1 year	0%	100%
1 year but less than 2 years	0%	100%
2 years but less than 3 years	0%	100%
3 or more years	100%	0%

Vesting shall cease on the date on which the Executive terminates employment with the Corporation, other than by reason of the Executive's death or disability.

B. <u>Acceleration of Vesting.</u> Unless the Option has earlier terminated or expired, vesting of the Option shall be accelerated so that the unvested portion of the Option shall become one hundred percent (100%) vested in Executive upon the earlier to occur of: (i) Executive's disability, as defined in the Plan; or (ii) termination of Executive's employment or service with the Corporation as a result of Executive's death.

6. Method of Exercise of Option. The Option may be exercised (in full or in part) by delivery of a written notice to the Corporation at its principal executive office, accompanied by payment of the Option Price for the Shares as to which such Option is exercised. [4] The Option Price of each Share as to which this Option is exercised shall be paid in full at the time of exercise, in cash.

7. Withholding. Upon exercise of all or any part of this Option, the Executive shall make arrangements with the Corporation for the withholding of any applicable federal, state and local income taxes. The Executive acknowledges that Shares will not be delivered until arrangements for satisfaction of any withholding tax liabilities have been made.

8. Expiration Date. Subject to earlier termination as provided in the Plan or this Agreement, this Option shall expire three (3) years after the Option Grant Date. Unless the Executive terminates employment by reason of death or disability, the Option shall [5] terminate on the date, which is ten (10) days after the date on which the Executive terminates employment. [6] In the event the Executive terminates employment by reason of death or disability, [7] the Option shall terminate thirty (30) days after the date on which the Executive terminates employment.

9. Shareholders' Agreement. As a condition of the exercise of the Option, the Executive agrees to execute a shareholders' agreement substantially in the form attached hereto as Exhibit A.

10. Agreement to Terms of Plan. By signing this Agreement, the Executive accepts the Option subject to the terms and conditions of the Plan and this Agreement. Unless otherwise provided in this Agreement, capitalized terms used in this Agreement shall have the meanings set forth in the Plan. As provided in the Plan, this Agreement shall be governed by, and construed in accordance with, the laws of the State of Delaware.

IN WITNESS WHEREOF, the Corporation, by its duly authorized officer, and the Executive has executed this Agreement.

Enterprise Systems, Inc.	Executive
By: ______________________	______________________
President & CEO	Signature

Analysis: Nonqualified Stock Options Agreement

1. **Undesirable Clause:** The agreement grants the executive nonqualified stock options, which favor employers and disadvantage executives. Larger companies with consistent profits generally prefer these plans because they are able to deduct the spread between the grant price and the exercise price as a compensation expense. Thus, employers tend to offer nonqualified stock options to rank-and-file employees, while reserving the tax-favored incentive stock options for a small cadre of top-level executives. The disadvantage of nonqualified options to an executive is that when he or she exercises the option, the difference between the grant and exercise price is taxed as income—even if the executive hasn't sold the stock and realized the income. Whereas, with incentive stock options, an executive is only taxed at the time the stock is sold, not at the time of exercise.
   Proposed Action: Inquire about receiving incentive stock options as opposed to nonqualified stock options, stating your concern that you will have to pay taxes in advance without having realized any cash gains.

2. **Undesirable Clause:** The vesting schedule is highly favorable to the company because it provides for a three-year, cliff-vesting schedule. Essentially, if the executive leaves the company for any reason, voluntarily or involuntarily, before the end of the three-year vesting period, he or she will forfeit all stock options, even if fired or laid off after two years and eleven months.
   Proposed Action: Negotiate an incremental vesting schedule that is significantly shorter in length, such as quarterly vesting, or at the least, annual vesting in equal percentage amounts equal to 33 percent per year. Your argument might be, "I am making a significant long-term commitment to the company and if there are circumstances that are out of my control, such as corporate lay-offs, I should not be penalized for those circumstances and forfeit the right to exercise a portion of my options based on my time with the company."

3. **Undesirable Clause:** In this provision, the problem is not with the language that is present but the language that has been omitted. Specifically, there should be an allowance for accelerated vesting of the options upon the sale or change of control of the company. As presently drafted, if the executive has been working at the company for two and one-half (2.5) years and the company becomes wildly suc-

cessful and is sold, he or she will still not have reached the three-year vesting period and therefore will not have a right to exercise any of his or her options.

Proposed Action: Request a "change in control" provision where your unvested portion shall become 100 percent vested if there is (1) a sale of all or substantially all of the assets of the company, (2) the sale of more than 50 percent of the outstanding capital stock in a non-public sale, (3) the dissolution or liquidation of the company, or (4) any merger, share exchange, consolidation or other reorganization or business combination of the company. This is more reasonable from your perspective; your core argument is that it's only fair that you participate in the upside if a favorable event transpires partly because of your contributions and hard work.

4. **Undesirable Clause:** Like the change-in-control provision above, an important clause is missing here. The company has omitted the cashless exercise provision. So, if the executive has 10,000 options and the exercise price is $10 per share, he or she would have to come up with $100,000 in cash, rather than temporarily borrowing the money needed to exercise the options by selling some stock to cover the cost of the remaining shares.

   Proposed Action: Request a "cashless exercise" clause, which is a slight modification to the current language. The last sentence should read, "The Option Price of each Share as to which this Option is exercised shall be paid in full at the time of exercise <u>(i) in cash, (ii) with Shares owned by the Employee, or (iii) any combination thereof."</u> Many exercise and sell simultaneously, using a cashless exercise clause.

5. **Undesirable Clause:** This is tricky. The option expires exactly three years after the option grant date. The executive will never have the opportunity to exercise these options, because they expire on the same date that they vest.

   Proposed Action: Carefully review your exercise and vesting dates to make sure there is at least one year's time differential from the time you are vested to the time you must decide to exercise your options. This will allow you to gauge the viability of this investment without having to make an immediate financial commitment.

6. **Undesirable Clause:** The options terminate ten days after the date on which the executive terminates employment. If the executive is fully vested, he or she will only have ten days to decide whether to make a

significant personal investment decision, while at the same time determining his or her next career move.
Proposed Action: Typically, ninety days is most common. It is reasonable to say something like, "I understand the company's interest in retaining its stock for current employees. With such an important financial decision, I'll need a slightly longer grace period, because my first concern will be getting another job and I want to make these personal financial decisions with a clear mind."

7. **Undesirable Clause:** The options terminate only thirty days after the date on which the executive terminates employment because of death or disability. Usually, in the event of a death, the family's immediate concern is with funeral arrangements; often, an executive's estate has to go through probate. By the time the family collects all the necessary information, these potentially valuable options will most likely have lapsed. If the executive becomes disabled (i.e., is in a coma or incapacitated), he or she should not be penalized with such a short expiration period.
Proposed Action: Typically, twelve months is used in these cases in order to provide the employee or the employee's family enough time to determine an action plan. This clause is especially important if the employee is fully vested and his or her options have real value, since this portion of the compensation may have functioned to provide ongoing stability and security for that individual's family.

Index

Glossary

accidental death and dismemberment (AD&D) a provision in a health insurance plan that pays a specific cash sum if an employee dies or loses a limb as a result of an accident.
Alternative Minimum Tax (AMT) an alternative calculation of income tax liability that the IRS applies to all returns. Sometimes individuals who, in a given year, have exercised stock options but not sold them are assessed additional income tax by virtue of the AMT.
arbitration the process through which a controversy is submitted to an impartial person called an arbitrator to resolve a dispute outside of the court system.
arbitration clause a provision in a contract providing for arbitration in lieu of a court action.
at-will employee an employee who can leave the employer, or can be terminated, with or without cause, at any time. In most jurisdictions, unless an employee has an employment contract, the assumption is that that person is an at-will employee.
benefits non-salary items provided to employees.
bonus a lump sum payment to an employee in recognition of reaching a particular goal.
cafeteria plan (also called flexible benefit plan) a benefit plan that allows employees to select among qualified nontaxable benefits; usually provides a basic core of benefits, such as medical and life insurance, plus a second layer of optional benefits.
cliff vesting vesting schedule where stock options vest incrementally after certain set periods of time—e.g., biennially, annually, quarterly.
commencement date the date on which employment officially begins.
compensation cap a limit on the amount of compensation an executive can receive.
Consolidated Omnibus Budget Reconciliation Act (COBRA) an act of Congress requiring, among other things, that employers with group health insurance plans continue to offer coverage to qualified beneficiaries in certain circumstances, for example, after the employee leaves the company. The health insurance provisions of COBRA only apply to employers with 20 or more employees.

co-payment a form of cost-sharing between policyholder and insurance company that requires the policyholder to pay a fixed fee toward the cost of each service used.

double trigger a combination of two events that triggers accelerated vesting of stock options. Usually, the first trigger event is acquisition of the company, and the second trigger event is the termination of the employee. Vesting only occurs if both trigger events take place.

employment contract a written agreement that outlines the services and pay arrangements for an employee. Employment contracts often also include sections related to the protection of trade secrets and confidential information, and sections that limit competition from the employee following separation of employment.

exercise to purchase shares of a company based on the terms of the stock option grant.

expiration date the date upon which a vested stock option can no longer be exercised and is forfeited back to the issuing company.

flexible benefit plan *see* cafeteria plan.

flexible spending account (FSA) (also called a reimbursement account) a system in which policyholders store up untaxed monies to pay for costs not covered under other benefit plans or for care for a child or dependent disabled parent. Individual accounts are funded with either flex dollars from the policyholder's budgeted balance, or with payroll deductions.

401(k) plan a cash or deferred arrangement allowing employees to use a fund for their tax-free contributions, and often their employer's contributions, which grows until the employee retires.

grant price (also called strike price) the per-share price, set by the company, that you pay when you exercise your vested stock options.

gross margin gross revenue minus cost of sales, which may include labor, shipping, third-party commissions, licensing fees, and inventory.

gross revenue total revenue that a company generates from the sale of products and services.

incentive stock option (ISO) a right to purchase a share of a company's stock at a particular time and price. Because of its tax advantages, an ISO can only be granted to an employee of a company.

incentive stock options agreement the agreement between the issuing company and its employee that governs the grant, exercise, and other rights associated with an incentive stock option.

net sales total or gross sales less all returns, discounts, amounts paid to third parties for license and application fees.

noncompete agreement an agreement not to work for a competing company for a specified period of time after leaving the current employer.

nondisclosure agreement (also called NDA or confidentiality agreement) an agreement to protect the confidentiality of information.

nonqualified stock option (nonqual, NSO) a right to purchase a sha of a company's stock at a particular time and price. Nonqualified stoc options are not tax-advantaged and thus can be issued to anyone; they are not restricted for issuance to employees as ISOs are.

nonsolicitation agreement prevents an employee, for a predetermine period after he or she leaves the company, from hiring any person wh was an employee with the company and from soliciting any of the com pany's current customers, clients, and near-term prospects.

options exercise period the period of time—after a stock option has vested but before the expiration date—in which the holder of the opti may exercise the option.

outplacement services corporate-sponsored programs designed to he individuals make workplace transitions, such as after layoffs, mergers, acquisitions, and relocations.

performance evaluation a structured formal interaction between a su ordinate and supervisor that usually takes the form of a periodic interview in which the work performance of the subordinate is examined ar discussed, with a view to identifying weaknesses and strengths as well as opportunities for improvement and skills development.

performance bonus a payment made to an employee based on achiev ing specified goals.

severance the continuation of wages and benefits after the terminatio of employment for a specified period of time.

signing bonus a one-time payment made to an employee when he or she accepts a job.

stock option the option to purchase stock at a time and price that you employer specifies.

strike price *see* grant price.

termination for cause a term used in employment agreements that ty cally allows the employer to fire the employee subject to the agreement for certain acts or inactions (insubordination, breach of confidentiality, commission of crimes) and excuses the employer from honoring any fu ther contractual obligations.

vesting period the period (typically two to four years) that must elapse before a stock option can be exercised.

M

N

O

T